Glimmer ON THE GLASS

JESSLYN RENE'E STREET

Library of Congress Control Number: 2016900774

ISBN: 979-8-88640-013-7 (sc)
ISBN: 979-8-88640-014-4 (hc)
ISBN: 979-8-88640-015-1 (e)

THE EWINGS PUBLISHING

One Galleria Blvd., Suite 1900, Metairie, LA 70001
(504) 702-6708

Contents

I dedicate this book
to every person who has felt pain
reach from behind you
unravel you,
chew you up,
and spit you out
only to leave you in the dark
but yet gave you the courage,
the strength,
to evolve
and seize your own
rainbow!

Every word is for you . . .

The real tragedy of life is to be succumbed by routine never meeting, never knowing, never becoming who you are to be or be who you are to become!

—JRS

Paradise

My Paradise . . .
A beautiful vision,
It always starts out the same
The sun glistening on every grass blade
I walk through the meadow
As the wheat weave between my fingers
The corner of my optic cavity
Glimmering with brilliance
From that golden solar plate,
Beaming from the sky,
The same silky coloring of my skin
Shining so brightly
Reflective in the eye of your ocean
Oh! How it peacefully fills me!
With every joy of the notion
This uplifting, freeing feeling
That my body
Comprehends with devotion
Echoing the words
Of unspeakable unbelievable love
As close as my fingertips
To a wing of a dove
. . . Paradise

Relax

I need to inhale
Then exhale
The negativity I'm feeling
Brain so drained
From this anxious feeling
HUSH!
Don't move . . .
Stop your pacing . . .

I can't stop moving
The emotion I'm feeling,
Is very consuming!
Intoxicating, in the worse way
It makes my stomach
Swivel and sway!

Just breathe . . .
Close your eyes,
Drift into serene
Sweet thoughts
Breathe life
Into the word
C A L M

Bittersweet

I saw you today
And you took my breath away
You literally
Made me speechless
Made my heart ricochet
Bounce off
The walls of my rib cage
Ignite that smile
I couldn't make stay
A glimpse in your eyes
Is all it took
You shook the world
All in one look
How couldn't I?
But really I can't look!
So bittersweet
I can't take that last glance
To watch you walk away
I can't put myself on that hook
That bittersweet moment
When my heart was took . . .

Soul Mate

As I close my eyes
and drift into darkness
Our hands touch,
under shadows kiss
We interlock our fingers,
as if they were our lips
Something feverish
and yet so beautiful
One can only describe as . . .
Bliss
An aura so magical,
It hovers over you like mist
Completely devours you,
Moves swiftly into you
Bringing all emotions to the surface
From the first sight of being curious,
From the first date of being nervous,
From the first kiss of being serious,
True love proved to be infectious
Awakening the immortal heart of me,
Proposing an equal,
of timeless infinity
Capturing love's promise
Making its fairytale true,
for you and me!

For Granted

There are things in this world that I can't even imagine
Living without you is one I can't even fathom
This is the worse emotion that I never wanna feel
In the life we live this is something inevitable to all
Something only God can heal
So I need you to know that I love you with all my heart
I have never taken you for granted
Mom, you are amazing!
You have the kindest heart!
We have a relationship with an unbroken seal
You taught me to love, you taught me to feel
You taught me forgiveness
Upon lesson after lesson
Having you as only MY MOTHER
Is beyond a blessing!
I have met women with broken souls
Who have lost touch of their children
Consumed by madness with no ambition
Women who have lost their mind after being dragged through hell
I don't know how you gained your strength
Or how you passed it to me as well
You are the reason in every single way
That I could be who I am
The baby girl you guided and raised
The young woman you gave legs to stand
I love you mommy
You are the beauty in my face
I'm so grateful to have you
You could never be replaced!

Barbed Wire

You pricked your finger
When you touched my heart
Vessels frozen from the abuse
Emotions torn apart
Seduced from love
A taste so tart
Visions so reckless
Your movements never smart
I swam through the ocean,
that you filled with mud
Showered in the water
that just became blood
Oozed like the puss
of a pimple pushed too hard
Became the corn on your feet
My emotions were scarred
I tremble at the thought
of this revolting life
Do I stay with you?
Condemn myself to this strife
To be born again . . .
How could I say no twice?
The angel within me won't come off that nice
Every single woman has her
sugar and spice
I loved you from the grain
I didn't have to suffice
You meddled with rubbish
Brought pain in my life
To paint you this picture
I would start with the tears that I cried
Then loneliness overwhelmed
and flooded my mind
It rained so hard

I was empty inside
No attempt to eat
Lost every appetite
Never been so skinny
I could blow like a kite
Never had I found evidence
of you doing wrong
But once you proved me right
I pulled the trigger on that gun
I exploded with anger
Venom in my lungs
Ran clear across the earth
Just to show you I'm strong
I leaped
as the phone connected
to the back of your head
Grabbed on to your body
and pounded until my knuckles turned red
started to gag
when I realized
It was you I was touching
Pushed you away
you stumbled to the ground
where you belong . . .
You are Nothing!
As I walked away screaming
I punctured my soul
on something
Was it metal?
plastic?
or the box cutter I'm holding?
But that young li'l bitch you wanted
claims she's got something coming!
I pace back and forth yellin'
"Bitch, I'm not runnin'!"
You crawl to me,
try to calm me down
and claim I'm not being the woman

That you fell in love with
I burst with laughter
so tickled I can't control myself
Screaming . . .
"This is exactly what you wanted!
A gangsta-ass bitch,
a loose pussy,
where all the boys fall in!
You wanted a selfish li'l girl
with dreams too far to grasp
when you had a woman
who loved you as if you were
first class!
You wanted a girl
who could proudly say . . .
"I fucked your bitch in your bed!"
Bitch, Are You Crazy?
Think about what you just said!
You wanted a female with no self-respect!
A female that couldn't give you nothing
That's the reason you crept!
I decided at this moment
I needed to take a walk
Kept the box cutter on me
Just in case that li'l bitch ain't smart!
I glided up the street
Thinking of everything that just went down
And just as the breeze hit me
So did all your fucking around!
How many places did I drop you off for this girl?
How many times did you watch me cry and felt nothing deep inside?
How long had you used me?
Watched by as my heart broke piece by piece
I granted every wish . . .
Thinking there was a beauty behind that beast!

But not anymore!
And never again
I had circled the block
Turned the knob on the door
Only to see you had fled
I searched angrily
For a phone
Some form of communication
To speak to a man I had just met
To hear the comfort of his tone
The wise words I knew he had
Then it occurred to me . . .
That you took it
Left me to stand alone
Against your li'l bitch's threat!
To shoot me!
A dead enemy's declaration . . .
"That cowardly li'l bitch!"
I screamed as I ran
Leaped off the porch
Sprinted as fast as I can
I knew you had to be limping
And couldn't have gone far
I reached the turn of a bend
Ran into a random
And had a thought!
Do I ask this random if they know you?
If they have seen where you had gone?
Before I could think on it longer . . .
"Hey, I know who you are!"
I turned around
I met random face-to-face
She said she had caught up with you
You had said your girl was crazed!
I laughed it off, then quickly explained
She cut me off and said
"All I'm gonna say is hurry as fast as you can!"
Sprinting across the intersection

I heard her say
"Beat that bitch ass!"
My laugh, I tried to restrain
I turned another corner
A pain in my side felt sharp
I rolled up my hoodie
To reveal scratch marks
Blood dripped from my side to the ground
My pace quicken
Feet fell hard on the ground
I hailed a car
To end this chase
The driver had asked if I was okay
I told him the truth
I had to get that phone
I giggled as I realized
It's like a dog and a bone
I caught sight of her
Told him this was my stop
God bless, I yelled back
Some real shit I never drop
I ran up behind her
Slowed my pace as an audience swarmed
So shocked I found her
Her expression conformed
"Strip!" I said
"Show me all that you got!"
She emptied her pockets
Revealing a lighter,
a bus pass,
and a prepaid phone . . . I never bought!
I turned to head home
She said a sentence that made me stop
"My mom wants us to come over for dinner"
I cocked my head to the side and said
"Bitch please!"
I wouldn't go to the moon with you
if you were on your knees

I left her there dumbfounded
As I made my way home
My mom picked me up
on the side of the road
I told her what happened
"Have you seen your face?"
I turn up the mirror
More scratches!
Just great!
We pulled into the driveway
I told her I would be back
When the phone hit her head . . .
It fell!
It broke!
It cracked!
I drove to the payphone
Dialed a number
I didn't know I knew by heart
When his voice answered the phone
My heartbeat from the start
I need to see you!
Can I come around?
Of course you can
I'll be waiting for the sound
Once I reached him
In his eyes I could see . . .
I had traveled through barbed wire
In order to find eternity!

Mr. Valentine

You make me feel . . .
Like I have something to hold on to
As if my world couldn't crumble
Because of you . . .
That undying love that runs in you
Evolves in your veins
And becomes you . . .
The oxygen you breathe
Because I need you . . .
Be anything possible
To relieve you . . .
No, I'm not mistaken I believe you
Nope, not one person could exceed you
The tenderness in your heart,
I couldn't leave you . . .
I'll say it again . . .
I know I need you!
To be with you on a romantic day . . .
Is too good to be true
You can be sure
I won't mislead you
or
Do anything to displease you . . .
In fact . . .
Let me please you
Be there for anything you need, boo!
This goes for every day
Not just Valentine's Day
Because I love you!

How You Do Me . . .

The moment I walk outside the door
That aching feeling gets me!
Makes me turn back around
To surprise you with kisses!
Feel you with me!
As if to have your fingers in between mine
That's how you do me . . .
Dipping in the well of divine
Oh, how sweet your lips taste
All of its purity
Raining down its symphony upon me
As if to sing to me
Oh, how I need your touch
As if you're not next to me!
Become one with my spine
As if to evolve with me!
Lay beneath your skin
As if to dissolve in me
That's how you do me . . .
Repeat it infinitely
Eternity and beyond
You and me
That's how you do me . . .
Making other lyrics obsolete
As if no one's here
Just you and me
Find every way . . .
To lose control with me!
Connected from fingers to toes
As if to attach to me
Keep me with you . . .
As if to dance with me!
Lose our hearts to each other
As if it were gravity
That's how you do me . . .
I said that's how you do me . . .

Unknown

Oh, what shall I write about
Let me think . . .
I'm pondering words
That just won't sink
Dabbling on words
That are cryptic to the ear
Serenading my thoughts
Manipulating my fear
Zooming in
To the point of destruction
Focal point
There's no interrupting
Blinded by sum
It's all or nothing
A few keystrokes
And I'm on to something
Filling in the blanks
With my nouns and verbs
Attacking with adjectives
Accenting my curves
Flowing with time
Like the age of my body
Hypnotized
Full-speed Bugatti
Wilding
Like the lotus inside me
Drop the world on ya
Effective rhyming

Glimmer on the Glass

Fixated
As the liquid sparkles
Cascading off the rim
Engaged
Remarkable
An audience takes wind
Of the twinkle
In our stars
Just as poetic
If not more than Lamar
Kendrick's
Justice to the Afrocentric
Living our life in the margin
As if the booth were sitting in
Is the college rule
From my seat to yours
Paper thin
Is how far I wanna be
Fixated again
As the liquid pours
The mountains we climb
Just to love you even more
The shadow caresses the glass
As the wine bottle we engorge
Lost in the glimmer
Butterflies from the core
Awakens from the eyelids
Of our children unborn
A fantasy of the truth
Proves infinite in our skies
Clink!

Go our glasses
As the solace flies
Impenetrable force
Of effortless time
Forever adored
And ever divine
Then fixated
As if
We are the light
From the heavens
That pirouette above their eyes
Glistening euphoric
More than words
To the wise
But yet
Fixated
From the glimmer
On the glass
As the liquid sparkles
Cascading off the rim
Engaged
Remarkable
That glimmer on the glass

Proud of Me

I wish I could unlock my mind
And seize that
Lost memory
See you
Sitting in your chair
Reading to LeeAnn and me
In your baritone voice
Reading other's words
Fluently
As if
It came from your heart
Out of your mouth
Straight to our ears
Of empathy
Wondering if I understood
The words
And their meaning
How attentive I must have been
Knowing it guided
My journey
How much sense it makes
To know that this
Was part of the connection
Of you and me
Furthering the result
Of respecting your words
Endlessly
Knowing that more
Than your stubbornness
Resides in me
How proud I am
To be one of
The Street Family . . .

In Honor of Ralph Lee Street, Thankyou for your strength, your wisdom, your courage, and your guidance, I Love you deeper than any words could describe.

LipStick

Lipstick

Shimmery
Brilliance
Lay across her lips
Sweet, soft pillows
Where honey drips
Shapely accurate
As if they were chiseled
Brain saturated
As your lip, you nibble
Reflex of a nervous
Tendency
Captured twinkle
From ear to ear
Unlocking the fragrance
Her lips adhere
So subtle
Yet so sincere
Gliding on the color
Lipstick you smear
Passionately absorbed
Warming the atmosphere
As she becomes the beauty
The mirror becomes fierce

Sometimes . . .

Sometimes I get scared
And feel the hurt and pain
That aren't there
How it hurts . . .
To be my worst enemy
Even seeing how much you truly care
My judgment becomes cloudy
My hearing impaired
Only feeding on the negative
When the positive got me here
How it hurts . . .
To think this is how you could be treating me
Almost as if I don't know you at all
So instead of knowing what I know
I act like I know nothing at all
How is it that when you hit the highest peak
On the mountain of happiness
It all crumbles . . .
Air filled with debris and rock
Smog rushes me
As I stumble
How can I soothe the pain
When a part of me knows that this is wrong
How can I trust what has lied to my face?
How could I ever trust at all!

How can I move when my heart is standing still?
Feel what I think and not what is real . . .
How will I never know what there is to know when what I know
might not be real . . .
All the answers you searched for
You already know
It's up to you to decide
If you can learn to let go
Let go of the past and reflect on the now
Follow the path that is paved
With your head above the ground
Travel the road where there is light
Go for what you're sure of
Let your heart dictate
What you already know of
Yes, you could be hurt
Yes, that is a result
But how will you know what there is to know
If you don't live the life that you got!

Mirandized Love

You have the right to remain
exclusive to my heart.
Anything you say or do
in your profession of love
will not be used against you,
even if we fall apart.
You have the right
to not be judged by me.
If you ever drop the ball
I'll help you get back
to the top of the key.
Do you understand
What these words mean?
With that in mind,
Do you wish to kiss me?

Crazy

I gotta try and fight the crazy
The crazy side of me
Stop myself from going over there
Even though all I want is your lips
Your lips on me
Whispering all of the world's wonders
From your lips to me
What I wouldn't give to hold you
And you believe me
When I say it's okay
Trying to find which words
Will make your mood sway
Not to mislead you
Just to show you the right way
Breathe life into you
Before we decay
Feel the warmth of your arms
Feel the tight grip on my hips
Indulge my lucky charms
More than your marshmallows
Are for me
Damn, just come and hold me
Let me show you how crazy this is
Oh, how it hurts when you scold me!
Got me feelin' so crazy
The rage is shaking
Fueling my power with my pain
As if I'm going super sane
The Kamehameha
Pours as it rains
And all that's needed to stop this
Is your embrace . . .
CRAZY!

From Silver to Platinum

Bubble gum wrapped
Like Nikki's Lamborghini
Safari on her side
Well, I got Kris McGee
Rubbin' on the lamp
Give me Aladdin's magic genie
Not dying to be Barbie
I'll settle for li'l sis Kelly
Give me enough to be comfortable
Enough to have Kandi Yams
Nails on file
Diamonds on my toes
Versace on my phone dial
$14.5 million home
Filled with my style
More than a bed to lay my head
Acres that stretch for miles
No animal control
Just control of the animal inspired
Letting stress go
Becoming the untamed wild
Breathing that effortless
No money stress breath
Paid to give the world
The beauty that I am

Yet judged for every character
Yet responsible for every line
Real is every bar from my larynx
As real as every bar and club you climb
Do Right And Kill Everything
As if the acronym for his name
Wasn't a sign
YOLO is a gift to everyone
Young Money doesn't waste time
Only if I could make millions
Off of every metaphor I rhyme
Me and Li'l Wayne
Could be conspirators
Of the same crime

Cliff-hanger

Hanging on to your every precious word
As time grows longer
We become fonder
Of your every mole
Of my every curve
Incredible magic
Speaking through your eyes
Hanging on to each precious verb
Creating a feeling
Creating a future
Never stop being your girl
Standing 360
Even as time grows swiftly
Surrounded by a love so fertile
Intense, quickly
Becoming the very essence
The very pure rarity
Of that dream within the dream
Something so young and fragile
But stronger than Achilles
Knocking me to my knees
The sweeping off the feet
Nervous giggles
By just eyes meeting in a gaze
Hanging on to each and every day
Loving tenderly
So courageous, it's brave!
Becoming the very epitome
Of night, noon, and day!
Hanging on to that moment

That You became I
That I became You
That We became Us
Astound
Wrap your head around the beauty of it all
Reaching for the heavens while you're touching the ground
SKYSCRAPER
Towering . . .
Like there's no one around
A love so high
It surpasses the clouds
Floating . . .
As if gravity were erased
Exhilarated
Remarkable trait
Caressing gentle love
On each note that you sing
Tantalizing the nerves in my brain
Soaked in your oils
Masked by your scent
Lost in my waves
Snug on my skin
Hanging on the cliff of
Forever and then . . .

Continuous Vapors

Can you see the vapors
Coming off of my body
The sensual vibes
That tingle inside me
Drifting smoke
Flowing out of my pores
Dancing in midair
Wrapping around my vocal cords
Suspending each thought
Undeclared
As it swirls into the depths of your lungs
Feeling the vapors
The sensual vibes growing strong
Toxic to your oxygen
Septic to your pores
Wild by nature
Waterfalls from each gorge
Filling each vessel
One drop at a time
One stroke of your hand
And you poison my mind
Manipulated by warmth
Succumbed by the thought
The strength that you hold
Our effortless love's plot
Influenced indefinitely
Silent are the
Tick and the tock
Relapsed by the heart
Vapors nonstop

Disappearing Act

I've been gone so long
You probably thought I was dead
But I guarantee
You ate the lies that were fed
No, I have no babies
No, I'm not with her
No, I'm not with him
Complicated was life
POOF!
Like I was never your friend
Cutting off the world
As if you could comprehend
The evil erupted
Every battle took wind
I used to wonder
If any of you
thought about me
Every Now and Then
But this isn't pills and potions
No longer
Can I overdose
On all your sins
The shadows surrounded me
The clouds darken
Cold was the feeling
My heart hardened
Thunder cracked
Making the ground rocket
On point was my guard
James Harden
Lighting unraveled
Like an active socket
Worn were my shoes

Empty was every pocket
The fog swarmed
Releasing an agent toxic
Collapsed were my lungs
A victim of Davy Jones locket
But yet I arose
Aimed and cocked it
Barrel of Fury
With an *X* on the target
Planted were my feet
22 Smith & Wesson
Nonstick
Survived by my foes
Latched onto their envy
As I
Became the tick
Whispers they left me
Every word caustic
I got the voodoo for you, bitches
illogic
Tormented
A bit nostalgic
But then again
They transformed
From innocents
To overcompensating dramatics
Until you make their brows rise
From that glimmer
Metallic

Two hands locked on the handle
A swipe of a finger
Hit the safety off switch
Aimed at your noggin
Cephalic
Pointer meets trigger
A tad barbaric
A li'l erratic
Absolutely manic
As the scene turns graphic
Bullet engraved, traumatic
As it enters the midsagittal plane
That's frontal . . .
Cranial damage
Hitting the scalp
Digging in the cranium
Obliterating brain tissue
Savage
Stopping in the occipital
That's your vision gone, bitch!
The end of your cabbage
Leave you lying there for scavenge
Disappearing from earth
As that's all you can manage
When my act of disappearing
Was far from average!

Music

Check it!
You're the speakers to my radio
The only voice on my stereo
You spit a track and let it go
Every song plays a scenario
Of where we been
Or where we dream to go

Baby, this is usual
We the couple that's unusual
The only girl that blows the notes
That the only boy plays on key
Piano

I could be a soprano
But the only gun in my holster
Is a G note
Now let it flow
From my flutes opening
Simpatico
I'll leave that on the bandstand though

Got me writing verses
On the verge of
Jhene Aiko
More along the lines
Of a never-ending dream though
We chillin' under the bungalow
I'm Juliet
You're Romeo
Future father
Of my embryo
I'm the colon

To your ratio
The CSI
To your Horatio
Made me fall faster
Than Domino's
Too bad it's DiGiorno's

Your music
Gives me that afterglow
As if it was
The first day of snow
Kiss you all day
No need for mistletoe
Be the Geppetto
To your Pinocchio
I'm video
You're audio
We're on the same note
Staccato
I'll be the Demi
To your Lovato
You're the Danny
To my Devitto
I'll be the Green
To your CeeLo
You're the music
To my Pandora yo

Magnifico
Urbano
Seduccion
Infinito
A mi Alma
La Musica
In case you didn't know!

Any Day

It could have been any day
But it was today
The day I could flap my wings
The day where all sadness washed away
The day where I let myself be free
Carried
Or whisked beyond a dream
In this desolate place
So far
Yet it fits in between
Reality and the fairy-tale scheme
Blown astray with the summer rain
Watch the sun sparkle
In the light of day
Released from the uniform
That fits my frame
It could had been any day
But it was today
Where I blew on a field of dandelions
And let all my cares drift away
I watched as they wander
Deviate
Veer

Took on the impression
Of Claude Monet
Sunset in Venice
Or Tulip Fields
Obsessed with the color
His art portrays
But at last
Caught in the web of freedom
Becoming hope's beacon
To that effervescent staircase
Leading to the most
Unimaginable
Magical
Epic
Exploration
Invention
Of my future's face
It could had been any day
But it was . . .
TODAY

Fatherless Child

I'm not a product of my past
I'm better off than my last
Prolific is my arsenal
Leaving folks staggering in my class
Virtue is in me
Something my father couldn't grasp
Father meaning male parent
Parent meaning
To be or act as a father to someone
I guess that wasn't you
Meaning withering away
As fragile as a bracelet clasp
Your name as awkward
As the rasp of an engine . . . Gasp!
As your exhaust fumes of bullshit
Comes straight from your ass
Excuse me as I figured we could be blunt
Your time for me has perished
Your double is the stunt
That Gemini in you
Just so ready to hit the blunt
But how far is the truth
When it comes to your runt
First daughter born
A slight bit salty
Could be perceived as scorn
But yet I am alive and grateful
But that's bread
To a different sandwich
On the next plate
On your neighbor's table
Crunchy are your words
Brief
Distasteful

Struggled to find the reasons why
But I'm just not able
It's a relief I grew up thinking
Being fatherless was an everyday thing
Seeing everyday mothers
Doing everyday things
Teaching their children to be
Kings and Queens
Showing a young boy
What a man really means
Teaching a young girl
There's more beauty
Underneath the unseen
Capable women
Beyond capable means
That rib in Adam's cage
What Eve really means
And all of us children
Hopefully for many things
The capital reason
To give a better life to our offspring
But back to you
And how effortless it is
For a phone to ring
Only for it to ring so much
When a correctional institution
Asks if you want to accept this call
You couldn't hold a glass
To how many tears you made fall
All because everything was about you
And your failure
You're the only one who made your time stall
So caught up in what life brought to you
When you are the reason
For every destructive path you caused
Let me highlight
I'm not angry
In my eyes you're absolved

I forgive you for your stupidity
I forgive you for having the thought
That me and some of my siblings
We're not meant to step foot
On the earth that were on
Clearly God saw through
Your scandalous pleasures
Unwrapped the knowledge
Of you being wrong
Though it took me a while
To realize any lesson you taught
I understand your purpose
On this earth believe it or not
The one thing you did successful . . .
Something you helped create more artistic
Than a backdrop
Beautiful
Intellectual
Musical
Lyrical
Luminescent
Children of Love
Who learned hopes and dreams
From their mothers
A human that stayed by their side
From bad dates
To temper tantrums
To belly rubs
Incredible
How many things can change
By someone just being there
All the weight you could have lifted
Off of these women's shoulders
But instead left a child to bear
How **incredibly** selfish of you
But let me underline
I'm well aware
And no sadness can cripple

The strength you gave me
For you being so scared
It's ironic that your age was a reason
And mine is the reason I don't care
See I could go deeper
Peel the skin back
Comment on subjects
On which you think
My memory lapsed
But that's cruel
Even though your sins lie within me
My mother raised no fool
But I will clarify one thing
I don't ever recall
Calling out for you, Father
You must have dreamt up such a funny thing
Though I do wish you peace
For the rest of your life
And pray you don't carry any more women
On your once-upon-a-dream scheme
No one needs that strife
No pain
No ignorance
No decades of lost time
How can you make up for something
When there's no VCR to press rewind?
I saw you awhile back
Doing a Cher
"If I could turn back time"
Asked for my number
As if to start off a new rhyme
And just like a VHS it gathered dust
Just another lie
I guess you were so caught up
In the latest family
Who cares if you leave
The first three behind

If jealousy is what you think this is
Then I guess you have been living your life blind . . .

My message to all the fatherless children
NO matter the circumstance
NO matter the situation
NO matter if his life was taken
You were not left behind
IF you survived yesterday
IF you survived today
You will survive eternity
Without him by your side
Heed his example of absence
And become a better man than he was
Even if he left this earth
Become the man he would be proud of
Marry a man who knows the true meaning of love
Don't let the past dictate your future
Fatherless is what fatherless does
Become the fatherless child
That soars high above!

Peephole of the Mind

Let me sit back and think
Of what I wanna give to the world
What sentences I say with emphasis
How to make the rubric
Bend and curl
Emphasize my swirl
On the alphabets
Rotation
Through the tongue
To lip movement
Of my voice's tone
Hella soothin'
From the earth
Soil that I am rooted
The soil to my spine
Through the mind's eyes
Of the movement in the skies
Clouds . . .
Caressing heaven's pillows
Soaring through the bright
Clear blue atmosphere
Reflective of the clearest waters
That just so captured
The same crystal ambience
That sparkles in your eyes

Let me synthesize
Break down the material
Of every hormone and chemical
Of two elements
To become unified
You and I
Step in and visualize
Through the peephole

Of what I'm seeing
And you will see
The unlocked treasures
Of what life has in store
Every prize
No need for the searching
The seeking
Of what's on the other side
To be your rib
Keep you standing straight
Keeping you balance
On earth
And outer space
Materialize . . .

To appear or become real
More than something you feel
Captured by the shutter
The iris of the eye
Placing that moment
Filed forever in your mind
Hypnotize
Induce hypnosis
Resembled sleep
Of some other kind
While I sit back and dream
Of what I wanna give to the world
Each sentence at a time . . .

Why Do You Make Me Cry!

Why do you hide your eyes?
Is it because you know you make me cry inside!
I know you have been around the block a few times . . .
But me and her don't coincide!
She's just an average chick, only along for the ride
So drop her off, pull to the side, open your trunk . . .
I'm what you see inside
That secret treasure that no one can find, secret lover somewhat divine.
I got your back, but you ain't got mine!
I'm the "pick up the lube and call you at 9."
See, baby, you left the trunk open one night!
I explored the horizons and there's oh so many lights.
I thought to myself, "Shorty, over there is lookin' kinda fine!"
But wait what's that tangle up my spine?
Oh yeah, that's right,
It's that silver leash you put on me 4 years ago in the line
Back when I thought you were the sweetest thing I could ever find!

Baby, you can hide your eyes, but you can't hide your heart!
Falling for these other chicks is what's tearing us apart!
I shielded you from the rain and protected you from the storm.
But when the lightning hits my chain, there won't be an us anymore!

I completed your every wish and even sealed it with a kiss, but your
lips are dirty, and I know I don't deserve this!
So I'm steppin' out the trunk and walking down the street.
Cuz your pimp game can't handle little ol' innocent me!

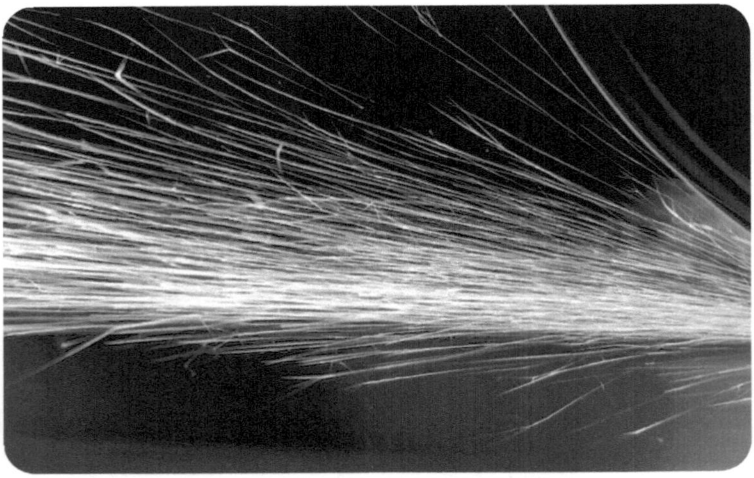

Revive

You revived me
Electrified me
Shocked my system
Set off sparks
Ricocheting inside me
Pulled out the paddles
Galvanized me
Sent 2,000 volts
To awaken the unconscious
State of my body
Lackadaisical
Without vigor
Lethargic
Brought me back to life
Frozen from the arctic
Laid there as if
I was Snow White in her coffin
Until love's petals
Brushed against my lips
Leaving a stain of blush
Attached to my skin
Generating heat
Locked deep within
As warm as the venom
Of a poisonous serpent
Only masked to reveal
The sweetest honey
Of pure love's first kiss
Unimagined
At first sight of your face
How intangible we would become
How each day we travel closer
To the Asgard of our outer space
As we build the Bifrost

By each step that we take
All of this . . .
Just because you looked my way
Sets off sparks in every socket
That lit up this place
Regaining strength in my pulse
As if it never escaped
Reviving a spirit so beautiful
So simple . . .
For two hands to create
Checking my vital signs
A love so relevant
That it predates time
Just one inhale
And I was revived . . .

Rejuvenated
Evolved
Vivacious
Impeccable
Voluptuous
Enthralled

I don't want this
To wear off
Let there be
No end at all!

Inconclusive

Doors
Closing
On what life
Has to offer
Amazing gift left,
Where light creeps under frame
Sadness fills her heart, where love
Still remains . . . Captured by feeling
Severed from umbilical love's chain
Door closed, perhaps to reveal chapter's end
Doors
Open
Gradually
After closing
To reveal what life
Has opened your eyes to . . .
Where light reaches pass your frame
Overwhelmed by joy and sadness
Life goes on with beauty and pure pain
Doors opened, revealing life's honest face

In Loving Memory of my grandma, Annie Mae Tomlin Street,
May 19, 1941-December 17, 2022.
May we see you again in everlasting paradise.

We Endure, For Tomorrow

Some people will live their lives
Without ever seeing the sunrise
Some people are so lost
When it comes to the concept of the mind
I got lost in a memory . . .

With my family ridin' through the Carolinas
My grandma saw a cotton field
And made my mom stop drivin'
She made us get out
So we could pick some cotton
Like your ancestors, she said
And a thought flew by, and I caught it
What would it had been like
To live in those days
Then I fall in a slip stream
And I'm trapped in a gaze . . .

I'd be in that kitchen
Hatin' that master
Being seen as a victimless slave
Being called out of my name
Just any ole property
Getting raped
No matter which floor
Which sheet
Which bed I lay
Beatin' to an inch of my life
For tryin' to flee
No matter which escape route I paved
Fortunate I am
For being born after
Slavery was abolished
Not like they could stop it

We had more goals to accomplish
The fact of the matter is
We all still discriminate against ourselves . . .
The color
The race
The gender
The straight
The gay
The heaven
The hell
The age
When one simple fact is true
You are my sister
You are my brother
On a different avenue
In a different state
In a different country
And just as God created me
He created you
How easy is it to get lost
In the evil sins of the mind
When looking at each other
We should only see the heaven
In each other's skies
But sadly we are lost
In the concept of the mind
How grateful I am
To be a mixed breed
Of a rare kind
Because the white in me
Loves the black in me
The Chinese loves
The Spanish in me
The Irish loves
The Trinidad in me
The Cherokee loves
The Chickahominy in me

The Turkish and Egyptians are kin to me
You can see all of these
On the skin of me
Close your eyes
And dream with me
Listen to the drums
Of my soul's orchestra
Beat infinitely
The violins strike their cords effortlessly
As the flutes and clarinets
Dance on a duet heavenly
The softness of the bassoon
Takes ahold of me
As I trip out of the slipstream
I let the thought drift away

I rub the cotton in between my fingers
And feel the sun hit my face
It's crazy how us people
As a whole have treated each other
It's a disgrace
The wind blows by me
As if I can hear
The whispers of the slaves
I kneeled to the ground
Running my fingers through the soil
Rich from the tears
They made rain
I could never imagine
Every pain they endured
I wished they could enjoy
The freedom in which I live today
If it wasn't for the stupidity of man
We would have a history
More brilliant than yesterday
The strength in their hearts
Is what made it possible
For US to walk

Among the earth this way . . .
Young
Old
Rich
Poor
Gay
Straight
Man
Women
Color-blind
We're all the same
If they could endure the tragedies of the past
Then we can endure the struggles
Of the future we face today!

Sensibility

Emotions
Swirling about,
Leaping from chaos
Connecting to heart strings
Nervous tangles, the cells brain
Fragile by feeble feeling
Playing effortless mind games
Thy capable of logic . . .
Clear sound reasoning
Thus, cannot survive without
Emotion creates
~sensibility~
Creates emotion
Without survive cannot, thus
Reasoning sound clear
Logic of capable thy,
Games, mind, effortless playing
Feeling feeble by fragile
Brain cells, the tangles nervous
Strings heart to connecting
Chaos from leaping
About swirling,
Emotions

Under the Stars

She stood there
Under the stars
Watching as they sparkled
If not brighter
Than the street lamp
Across the pavement from her
The atmosphere fell cold
Though no goosebumps
Lay across her skin
She exhaled and her breathe
Danced in the wind
She marveled at their brilliance
The twinkle of Orion's Belt
The slide of the Milky Way
The drink of the Dipper's cup
She wondered if she could
Possibly somehow join them
In the beautiful night sky
Just as Frigga's spirit took its place
In the blanket over their eyes
A beautiful death one cannot deny
As she gazed at its beauty
Reflective in her eye
"If only I had that choice," she thought
Wrapping her sweater closer to her torso
Watching as the wind
Gathered fall's leaves behind her
Creating a whisper
Symbolic to the wish
Of her silent thoughts
She took one last glance
Fantasied by its ambience
Almost as if to step off into its radiance
Closing her eyes
She felt lifted by the carriage of the wind
And at that very moment
She knew she was destined
To be
Forever Under the Stars . . .

Crashing Tides

She was awakened
By her iPhone's alarm tone
Like any other morning
It was time to get on the road
She unraveled herself
From his naked body
Entered the closet
Found her red satin robe
Victoria's Secret
Nothing shoddy
Grabbing her towel
She turned the knob slowly
Hoping not to awaken
Her sweet love cannoli
Entering the bathroom
She disrobed, turned on the shower
And let the steam fill the mirrors
Stretching, as if to embark
On the new day's adventures
When really . . .
It's just another day at work
A new day's sutures
She let the warmth of the water
Take hold and capture her body
Filling her lungs with the intoxication
Of a lustful memory
The shower water pushed against her
As her eyes shut
Taking her mind back to the Pacific Ocean's rush
The waves crashed together
Guiding the young couple deeper
And deeper into its abyss
Wrapped are her legs around his
As he balances against the north tide wind

Cradling her body ever so tightly
Against his sea-salt-stained skin
Positioned to face each other
Locked in each other's gaze
With nothing and no one around
Surrounded only by love's ocean
Their noses touch
Indulging in an Eskimo kiss
A slight tilt of the head
And the couple part lips
Tracing each other's outline
Attached from . . .
Head to shoulders
Hands to hips
Knees to ankles
Toes turn into fins
Euphoric as the sunset
Kissing the sea on the horizon
Naturally beautiful
Naked as the skin
They swim in . . .
As the water turns cold
She collapses out of her memory
Just as fast as she fell in
Turning the knob to hot
Hoping to start the memory
All over again!

That Day We . . .

On the day that we met!
As the half of our world pushed its doors shut . . .
I caught sight of you in mid strut . . .
As if the world's clock had reset.

Absorbed by a gaze I'll never forget . . .
Lost, I had been consumed by a rut.
On the day that we met!
As the half of our world pushed its doors shut . . .

I was an animal caught in your net!
I was suffused with a great power that lies in my gut!
Just as action found me, the revolving door came after the director yelled cut!
Love's grasp held tighter than a corset!
On the day that we met!

The Weeping Willow

The breeze gathers in her branches
Though her leaves are concrete still

The breeze gathers in her leaves
Though her bark has a ridged will

The breeze rushes against her bark
Though her roots are bound and sealed

The breeze rushes against her roots
Though she's absent, unable to feel

The breeze stops . . .
Though the wind echoes the word "kill"

The breeze pushes the vines
To wrap around her trunk, hoping she will heal

The breeze prays that one day
The weeping willow will once again become real

Compass

I found myself in an open field
Three more steps, I couldn't help but yield
The perimeter is dark all around
If I'm not lost, I won't be found
Who will hear my heart?
When it hits the ground
Its last beat's echo
Silence all around
You could hear me tremble from behind
Pounding deep against my spine
Is there any need, moving on
I'm out in the open
Miles far beyond
Is there any hope at all
Just feet on the ground
With no time to stall

I look up
The compass appears
Lighting the way
Under heaven's stairs
While my world is crashing right behind
East looks pretty bleak
North a long, long stride
West an exit not too far behind
Take it and risk it all
Be there to catch me
Don't let me fall
Is this the way . . . or naw
I'm out in the open
Be my guiding light
Am I living thy purpose
Golden Compass clear of my sight

I woke up . . .

I arose
Becoming higher
And higher
I became the dawn
The first period of light
My arms carry an ambiance
That shines on
And on
Orbiting
Revealing everyone
I awoke . . . The Sun

I sprouted
From the soil
Rooted beneath me
As the sun cascades on me
You'll see my nickname
Speaks for me
"Lion's tooth"
Much more graceful
Than threatening
Until a li'l hand
Tears me from my roots
Closes its eyes
Making a wish
Upon a dream
Blowing all the seeds
Off my head
I awoke . . . A Dandelion

I molted
Metamorphosis
A nymph from my larva
Metamorphosis

Greek are my ancestors
Though uneven, in the strict sense
My wings take flight
In a feverish sweat
I often like to lie
where the grass is still wet
Reflective is my sight
As the sun feeds my fire
Growing like the seed
I sprung right out of . . .
I became alive
I awoke . . . A Dragonfly

I shed
Removed it all
All of my skin
Naked is my body
Clear as my eyelids
My neck elongated
Like the rays of the sun
An egg I came out of
Like the seed where I began
Slithering as I am legless
A creature where my wings
Are all gone
Camouflaged
By my serpent scales
I awoke . . . A Snake

I roar
Possessing
Both beauty and strength
Second largest cat
To grace this earth
Fur coated the color of honey
Pride reflected in the sun
Exposed
Nocturnal

I take flight at night
As if I still had my wings
As silky as the snake
Ambushing my prey
Queen of hunting
A seed given from grain
I awoke . . . A Lioness
I descend
Breaking free
Leaving the womb
The sun kissed my face
As the dandelions bloom
Morphing like a dragonfly
Shedding my skin
Like the snake
Grounded
As her lioness
Pure honey
Leaves the lipstick to trace
Consumed by passion
Absorbed by affection
Adam's rib replaced
I awoke . . . A Woman

Honey Bun

Our conversations
Were like silent whispers
Carried off by the wind,
In the night's sky
No one knows what they consist of
No one but you and I

The thought that we
Would be parted forever
Was unthinkable
Unfathomable
A tragedy felt by
No one but you and I

The most riveting,
Excruciating pain
A dictionary can't even describe,
It felt like suicide
As we died in each other's arms
No one but you and I

It wasn't our choice,
I can't even lie
As the days moved on
The only strength I had
Was used to cry . . . Your tears and mine
No one but you and I

Silly little things
Would make tears pour
From my eyes
A beautiful song I wanted to sing
Only meant to end your cries . . . And now mine
No one but you and I
Your heart will forever beat with mine
As if we were never untangled but intertwined
Created from the dough
He is your cinnamon
I am your butter
Your our Honey Bun
No one but you and love

Naive

Native to being naive
I understand what you mean
Giving all that you are
Giving all that you mean
How the thread works through the seams
Never mind how
The story changes behind the scenes
The curtains rising
The backdrop is falling
Showing what's underneath the unseen
Creating a monster
Only seen in the movies
But hella real
When you come face-to-face
With the enemy
Naive to the Goonies
Excuse me?
Can you get your camera out this scene!
What an amateur . . .
He doesn't even know the plot of the story
Never mind that he's in the way
Of the climactic scene unfolding
Like the crease in your
Light blue jeans
Torn like the rip on your knee
Life just isn't what it seems
Hits you at the joints
Stretches your tendons
No matter how hard you fight

It still brings you to your knees
Leaving you and you alone
To find or create
The courage to dust off your own feet
Never mind that you had to be naive
Started from the bottom
Just to figure out . . .
Well yeah, I do believe
Preaching next to Nas
Like "I know I can . . .be what I wanna be!"
And at the same time
It's just so damn scary
Living your life now knowing
There's no more time to be naive!

Dual Blades

She stood there gazing through the blinds
At a sight that was hard to see
There's was no need to read between the lines
It was a picture-perfect scene from the movies
There she stood one story high
In his darkened room gazing down at the street
Pointer finger stuck in the blinds
Though her knees were meant to buckle
Collapse, right underneath her feet
But yet she stood there without a blink of an eye
Absorbing every movement made
Absorbing how the sun hit the car
And cascaded off of this white girl's face
Absorbing him seated as a passenger
The shade slightly covering half of his face
Shock ricocheted through the valves of her heart
As she watched a smile drift onto the girl's face
Inch by inch their lips crept closer
Closing the silhouette of their vase
Pain crept into her heart
Which soon overflowed with rage
She backed away from the window
Grasping at the metal in her purse
Something to light up the stage
Something to bring to him a curse
She stared at the knife's scorpion emblem
Caressing both pieces in her hands
Attaching them together
She undid each blade and quickly took a stand
Two steps toward the window
Her finger back in the blinds
Gazing down at the street
Watching
Feeling the adrenaline climb

They exited the car walking toward the building
Her back against the wall as she glided
Room to room
Darkness filled the apartment
The dual blades . . .
In her right hand, behind her back
Gripped close to her spine
She peered out the peephole
Attaching voices to their faces
As the hallway burst with sound
Him and his homeboys
A squeaky voice filled with laughter
Belonging to her no doubt
He said he would be just a min
As he put the key in the door
She stepped back into the closet
Adjacent to where he stood
Sucking in the cry she wanted to let roar
Light creeped from the doorway
He turned around to lock the door
She waited for him to reach the living room
Before exiting where she stood
Stepping lightly
With every effort that she could
Her feet leapt off the arm of the couch
In one swift movement, the blades were at his neck
With her legs pretzeled around his waist
The other hand lay across his forehead
"Give me one good reason why I shouldn't kill you right now?"
She said with clenched teeth
"Give me one good reason why I should let you live?"
he said smoothly but sweating like Keith
Before she could drag the knife across his neck
He reached for the back of her shirt
Slamming her to the floor
Dual blades flying under the table
No time for her to scramble
He laid heavy punches to her core

She knew it was a gamble
Her innocence was overpowered
This isn't the first time for sure
Knocked unconscious, she lay sprawled on the carpet
He walked out the apartment as if nothing happened at all
Not a ripple in his hair
His head held tall . . .
. . . 18 minutes ago . . .

She stood there gazing through the blinds
At a sight that was hard to see
There's was no need to read between the lines
It was a picture-perfect scene from the movies
There she stood one story high
In his darkened room gazing down at the street
Pointer finger stuck in the blinds
Though her knees were meant to buckle
Collapse, right underneath her feet
But yet she stood there without a blink of an eye
Absorbing every movement made
Absorbing how the sun hit the car
And cascaded off of this white girl's face
Absorbing him seated as a passenger
The shade slightly covering half of his face
This is the moment she thought
This was her saving grace
She gathered her belongings
And ran to the door
She took the spare from under the mat
And locked it secure
She ran to the laundry room without looking back
Ran to the last dryer
Kneeled down and leaned her back against the wall
She listened as he entered the building
She heard a female's laughter
Followed by a couple of guys' uproar
He said he would be just a minute
She listened as the apartment door shut

She could hear his footsteps enter each room
Searching for her she presumed
It fell silent for just a moment
Then the footsteps continued
The door flung open hitting the wall
Come on in, he said
They entered as his guest
As she, his victim fled
Once hearing the door close
She immediately ran for the exit
The sun hitting her face
She was blinded by her own reflection
Staring at her face in his car
She was blinded by deception
She pulled out the dual blades
That lie in her purse
A present he had given . . . What a suggestion!
Made her way around his car
Scratching off paint . . . What a deflection!
Slashing each tire on the way
Not quite her rage in projection
Satisfied with her work
She tore free to the back of the building
Finding a new way home
Was worth the courage she was building
The minute you get that sight of freedom
You take it and never look back
Lying sprawled on the carpet
Will only continue with each slap
Break away and find yourself
Create an eternity
For if you stay with him
Your end will be a deadly defeat . . .

In the Pocket

This guy has got her . . .
Prince Royce
Stuck on a feeling
Someone catch her
Her head's floating to the ceiling
Blushing from smileys
Emoji healing
Trapped in his pocket
Her heart, he is stealing
Anticipating,
Each message he's sending
Hurry up, boy!
Before the smile starts fading
Yet she's stuck in his pocket
And no one knows why
This feeling, she's feeling
She cannot deny
I told her, "It's love . . ."
She said, "Girl, you a lie!"
I'm telling the truth
It's that look in your eyes
That butterfly effect
Has you on cloud 9
Negative the drug
You can never be too high
You're stuck in his pocket
And you can't even explain why!

Light Blue Jeans

If I could be anywhere
Like right . . . right now . . .
I would be in a meadow
Lying under dozens of clouds
You would be next to me
Millions of daisies all around
Birds would be chirping
Zephyr with every sound
I would be sitting Indian-style
Wearing my light blue jeans
White tank top
Flip flops a little torn at the seams
Leaning my head back
Looking at the heavenly sky
Talking to you
Letting time travel on by
Smiling
Laughing
Seeing that glint pass from your eye
to mine
That would be plenty
I'm talking one of a kind
Not even thirsty
Not even a nibble on my mind
Full from happiness
Full from delight
I'm talking standing in the sun
Olivia Pope

A full life of beauty
A full life of hope
What is pain?
What does it mean to cope?
These are the questions
That are farthest from the coast
Yup!
That's where I would be!
Sitting right there . . .
In my light blue jeans
White tank top
Flip flops a little torn at the seams
Right where life is grand
Where we will live by any means . . .

Into the Darkness

There has been a lapse of time
Where darkness found its way in
It didn't seep through the door cracks
It just burst right on in
With no invitation
With no hesitation
Just picked a chair
Made itself comfy
And dove right in
Went to the kitchen
Made itself some coffee
So its rage kept expanding
It went room to room
So we had no choice
But to soak it all in
It evaporated happiness
So the rain would pour right in
The rain flooded us entirely
There was no way out
We were all locked in
Succumbed by the devil's thoughts
We just slipped and fell in
Until new victims came about
Stuck in the devil's kettle

We couldn't reach the spout
A smog swirled around us
Gassy fumes plummeted out
Virion surrounded us
Guarding the only way out
Until we evaporated ourselves
Right out of the kettle's mouth
Back in solid form as if it were a dream
The darkness crept away
Leaving the mirrors fogged with steam
It slowly drifted away
Without any notice
Without a goodbye
And suddenly the light of day
Took over every inch of the sky

S.I.U

Posing when ready . . .
Click!
Taking pictures hold steady . . .
Click!
Capturing that angle
Just for you
Undoing anything tangled
Unraveling the true me to you
Giving away that moment
No one ever sees but you
Gazing upon my portrait
Glued to your lens
Earth's orbit
"Yeah, that's me looking at you!"
Just one . . .
Click!
And all the sudden . . .
Click!
I've fallen in love with you
Caught underexposed
All alone in a dark room
Developing a chemistry
Sinking our teeth in . . .
Consumed!
Painting that smile . . . J-U-S-T . . . right!
Letting you know
Click!
That I am . . .
Click!
So Into You

Blown

As if a frown was permanently painted
Upon thy face
Scattered like the debris
That surrounds this place
Limp . . .
No muscle in thy pocket
In which to draw an ace
All obstacles left waiting
Hesitating before the start
Countdown to the race
Contemplating . . . pulling hair
Focus misplaced
1 . . .
Courage to start the engine
Clearing out every space
2 . . .
Emptiness trying to fulfill
Each question of this case
3 . . .
Pressing the gas
Letting go, igniting the chase
Blown by the struggle?
Well, it's time to set thy own pace!

R.O.M.L

I miss you like there is no tomorrow
My heart is filled with your love
And plenty of sorrow
What I wouldn't give to have you back
There's no life I can borrow
Infinite cries filled with pain
I can assure you they surpassed morrow
Every single day's endless tears
Come July 19th no claro
For the rest of my life
I will miss you like there's no tomorrow

Overflowing

Words pour out
Swelling from your throat
Vomiting concepts
Too shy to be wrote
Rambling the subconscious
Spilling the absurd on your coat
Shedding pure feelings
While looking for the solution
In your tote
Blinded by emotion
Adrenaline fueling your boat
Try to stop the tears
Before they fill up the room
And you float
Laying the blame on yourself
Digging your own moat
Quick to snap on anyone
Willing to open their mouth and gloat
"Pain will swallow you whole
But happiness will let you go . . ."
End quote
Sabotaged by the vomit
Overflowing from your throat

The real cookie

The Half-Baked Story

Lost in a dream
Wishing it were life
Cookie rolled out of bed
Stretching her arms to the sky
Pulling her hands to her face
She began rubbing her eyes
She glanced at the clock
Before running out the room
Overslept again
No alarm to hit snooze
She slipped while racing from the shower
She cut on the light
Just to lose power
Profanities leaped right off of her tongue
She scrambled around the room
Where had her uniform gone?
She flipped over the mattress
She rummaged through her clothes' basket
Each shirt had a stain
Each stain
Changed the color of the fabric
Frustrated, she listened
As her stomach growled with havoc
She slid on a T-shirt
That would make the dress code frantic
Sliding down the banister
She wiped out!
Face first . . . planted!
Up on her feet, rubbing her knee
She stumbled to the fuse box
Flipped the switch
"Man, I'm famished!"
Limped to the kitchen
Empty were all the cabinets

Tore open the freezer
One toaster strudel . . .
With no icing packets
She put it in the toaster
And waited, laying her head on the counter
A couple of minutes went by
And no sound from the toaster
She sprang from the chair
To check out the problem
It wasn't even plugged in
The cord was tangled at the bottom!
She plugged it in and fled to her room
Put on her shoes
Tied up her hair
Where was her coat?
More time was consumed
"There it is right under the vacuum!"
Grabbing her keys, she flew down the stairs
Walked in the kitchen
The toaster sparked flares
She found the extinguisher
And put it right out
Pulled out the strudel
Black and bubbly
As if it had gout
She threw it in the trash and walked out the door
Got in the car
Drove down the street
The engine began to rattle
She pressed the gas hard
One pedal, two feet
The car came to a stop . . .
Dead in the street
She got out and pushed
Merging car horns beeped
"All right! Okay! I'm moving out of the way!"
Next thing you know, thunder cracked
It began to rain
"My, oh my, this is not my day . . ."
Cookie made it to the curb

Closing the door, she locked her keys in
There they were lying in the ashtray
Shaking her head
She dug through her purse
Searching and searching
Feeling the worse
Just as the rain turned from sprinkles
To golf balls instead
The image of her cell phone plugged into the wall
Was pasted to her head
She walked further seeing a bus stop ahead
And here comes the bus
She took off like lead
Almost to the bus stop
She turned and . . . Kur plop!
The bus went on by
Splashing her with the biggest puddle
That fell from the sky
All she could do was STOP!
Now she was drenched from head to toe
Water squished in her shoes
She left her socks at home
"What is the point? Why should I even go!"
"Well, I have come this far . . . just a few blocks to go!"
She trudged along on the side of the road
15 minutes later
She was at her job
Swung the door open
Pulled up a chair to let off a load
"Hey, Cookie, what happened to you?"
She looked up at her manager and said, "Aaaaaa chooo!
I'm sorry, I'm sorry I overslept
I slipped out the shower,
I slid down the steps,
I bumped my knee,
I bumped my head,
The lights went out,
The toaster was on fire,
I swear, I swear I'm not a liar!
The strudel was black,

My car broke down,
By the way, I locked my keys in"
"No Diggity?"
"No Doubt!"
I left my phone at home
I'm soaking wet!
I tried to catch the bus . . .
But it caught me instead!
All my uniforms were dirty . . .
Cookie opened her coat, and her shirt read . . .
"They Say I Act Like I Do Not Care. I Tell Them I Am Not Acting."
With Donald Duck on the side
I walked all the way here
My shoes are squishy inside
I trashed my room . . .
"But wait a minute, Cookie . . .
I'm sure you know . . . I assume?"
"What is it?"
She laid her head on the counter
Cookie felt distressed
She had no energy . . .
She needed rest!
"It's Wednesday!"
"Yeah . . . So!" She muffled through her hair
"Cookie, you're off today!"
Cookie popped her head up
Then she looked around
She laughed hysterically
She fell to the ground
"Wait just a second, don't go away . . ."
She brought out a delectable chocolate soufflé
"This will carry all your burdens away!"
"Thank you. As you see, it's been such a crazy day!"
As she cut it with the spoon . . .
It sunk right in
"This has been such a Half-Baked Day!
That's what kinda day it's been!"

The Heart

They say the heart is a complicated thing
When true love really resides in your brain
It's the oxytocin
The hormone secreted from your pituitary gland
Makes you fall in love so fast you stumble, not stand
It appeals to the neuroanatomy of intimacy
Like holding one's hand
Brushing hair out of one's face
Wanting to truly understand
But perhaps love can really be felt by the heart
Its beats are so strong
It keeps us from falling apart
The main purpose to give us a life
Or arguable supplies oxygenated blood to our organs
While taking unoxygenated blood to the lungs to be oxygenated
But when you hear an artist speak of the heart and love
You never hear about its . . .
Four chambers
Three layers
Four valves
You see its colors
You feel its pound
You taste its sweetness
You hear its depth
You smell its buttered dough rise
On its breath . . .
And that my friend really explains why
Without a heart your brain would die
And this silly little thing called love
Would not exist
Our whole entire world would be in paralysis
But yet the brain is oh so smart
It taught us to love with the heart

Nightmare on Dream Street

(The Temptress Part 1)

The scenery was grim
Cold was the night
Charcoal, the color of the sky
Smog lay 3 feet off of the ground
SILENCE
Not a peep, not a sound
There lay a body
Just off of the curb, on the street
A white woman in her late twenties so it seems
A brunette, her hair the length of her face
Blue were her eyes
Her fingerprints erased
Pink chipped paint on her toenails
Under her fingers . . . dirt and epithelial cells
There she lay naked
Not a cloth, not a cover
Stranded in the darkness
Who did this?
A stranger? A lover?
No ligature marks
A struggle for sure
Held against her will?
Did she open the door?
Blood stained on her lips
A bullet through and through
Taken by her chest
Knife wounds by the dozen
The ME would have to tell us the rest
Detective Anderson walked up Dream Street
Spotting a neon light at the corner

Belonging to The Tavern,
Inside disarray,
Clearly out of order
He knocked a few times
Just to see if anyone was there
Out came a li'l old lady
White streaks in her hair
"I'm sorry, ma'am, for disturbing you at such a late hour . . ."
"Have you noticed anything strange tonight
That might have transpired?"
"Did you find a body there . . . There at the end of the street?"
"Yes, ma'am . . . I'm afraid we did."
Detective Anderson pulled a phone from his pocket with the victim's face lit upon the screen
"Do you know this woman, ma'am?"

She stared for just a moment
Then quickly turned away
"Yes, she got in a spat with my bouncer . . . She made quite a fuss!"
"What do you mean?"
"She threw glasses everywhere . . . knocked over several chairs!"
"Do you know her name, ma'am?"
"No, sir . . . I'm afraid not!"
"Where can I find the bouncer?"
"I believe he went home . . . Apartment 82, Rem Court. By the way, his name is Gus!"
"Just one last question, ma'am . . . Do you remember anything else from tonight that could help us?"
"All I know is that Gus called her . . . The Temptress . . ."

Apple Pie

Erotic scents from the oven
Scents so fragrant, I am lovin'
Cinnamon apples, tons of crumbs
Warmth on every spoon, golden crust
Every bite full of intense lust
Impeccable taste, high-pitched hums
Savory with a glass of milk
Rolls off of your tongue just like silk
Pure heavenly treat yum, yum, yum

Praying Mantis

Praying mantis lands on me twice
Right on top of my head, how nice!
She flew off, putting up a fight
Landed next to me, arms up straight
As if to defend her soulmate
Her movements swift as fast as light
Her knees were bent, steady, precise
One summer day, sugar and spice
Nature's beauty right in my sight

Hookah

What is the length of your travel?
What is the depth of your footstep?
The world is just the base to his hookah
While the clouds to us is just smoke in the sky
Swirling ever so high
Just gazing in the sky
Flowing on the breeze
As if the heavens lay on the clouds
Infamous beauty
Just pulling out your chair
And putting you at the edge of your seat
Filling you with words
Words that you dare not speak
How real is this?
You and me
Sitting under our destiny
Traveling this path that we just can't see
Leaving it all to our toes and our feet
Pushing on that gas pedal
To somewhere
Anywhere
Everywhere
Effortlessly
Positively flying high
Leaving our footprints on the earth
Branching out so the universe
Will recognize our worth
Showing that unity starts at birth

Everywhere and anywhere
Beyond this earth
Showing that our travel
Is deeper than our step
Longer than the strength of our arms
Bigger than the hookah
That produced the cloud I'm lying on
More than smoke
But the pillow that keeps us off of the ground
One day we will be more than comfortable
We will ascend
We will be profound

Skittles

Flavors run wild
With one taste of your lips
Filling the room with color
Passion-absorbed fingertips
Painting their swirls
Holding my hips like this
Seeing your soul carry mine
Gripping my fingers ever so tight
Whispering sultry words
Now pulling at my wrist
Perspiration glistening on your forehead
Raining dew on my back
Kiwis quenching your thirst
Oranges are my strawberries
Making stars full with cherries burst
Strong is the friction
Becoming one of a kind
The walls can't contain
This love of mine
What is one room . . . ?
To such a beautiful world
Just . . . like . . . that . . . boy!
Mmmmm . . . Damn, girl!
Accenting each canvas
With every sweet sound
Grapes of all colors
By your fruits I am bound
Bended and twisted
In formations unfound
Uncommon, our tornado
No boundaries is our length
Addicted to the feel
Tangy
Ripe
Unpeeled

Feathers is your hair in my hand
Burrowing your face
In my coconuts
Round
Full
Tanned
Drinking their nectar
Nipples you can't withstand
Gripping your arms
Swinging on your banana branch
Erupting our own rainbow
Like a volcano
But much more out of hand
All a quiver is my body
As you ignite the earthquake
Pulling my hair
Biting my neck
All of a sudden your voice shakes
Crashing together
Slowly gliding on the hurricane
Drenched is our bodies
Stained are the sheets
Devouring each Skittle
Our bodies release
Tasting the most . . .
Unforgettable
Unshakable
Unimaginable
Flavor of all
Our eyes roll back
Saturated on each bud on our tongue
Is love . . .

Nightmare on Dream Street

(The Temptress Part 2)

About 30 minutes later
Detective Anderson found blood splatter
At the bouncer's door
He pulled out his gun and flashlight swiftly
BANG! BANG! BANG!
"Gus O'Brennan, this is the police. Open up!"
Detective Anderson waved his flashlight toward the window
Again, the place was in disarray
The window was cracked
A smell caught Anderson's attention
It was the smell of decay
With one whiff of that, he kicked down the door
The smell tainted his memory
It ate at his core
He entered slowly
Sweat dripped from his brow
The scene looked all too familiar somehow
An Irish terrier lay in a pool of blood
Glass scattered all over the place
Furniture ripped
Feathers spilled everywhere
Blood-stained pillow case
He checked each room
Finding an assortment of things
A box of a grill stick matches
Burnt at each end
A blood-stained parrying knife in the kitchen
Ice rink blue Valspar paint
Filled the entire tub in the bathroom
A toxic scent hit his nose
Bleach, he assumed

He followed the scent with his nose
gun still in the air
His flashlights dim glow
Caught sight of blood on a doorknob
A cool breeze drifted from under the door
Blood drop formations on every other stair
From the design of Gus's apartment it would appear
He was not just its occupant
But its landlord
As Anderson reached the bottom
There was a mixture of smeared blood and paint
He followed its Crimson ice rink waves until they disappeared
Right under yet another door
He turned the knob slightly
Held his breath
As bleach consumed the air for sure
There lay Gus naked at the top of the cellar steps
One leg twisted
One foot caught in the cellar door
Dozens of burn marks on his lips
His hands
His testicles
His chest
Anderson reached for his walkie
And called it right in
If there was anything he was sure of
This had to do with the temptress!

In Loving Memory of Mystic, Xiang, and Slipper.
I wish we could have stayed here forever.

In the Middle of the Moon and the Sun

I sit in my nature
I sit in my dwelling
Taking in the trees' oxygen
With my umbrella sailing
Gliding in the wind
Two eagles soaring in the distance
Black stallion on my left
Polar bear at my back side
Hyena on my right
Indulging in the sun's effervescences
While lying in the shadow cast by the moon
Effortless beauty encounters us
Not one minute too soon
A gust of wind moves with ardor through blades of grass to my cheek
Feeling the hitch change as my voice speaks
"We should stay here and never leave . . ."
Right in the middle of the moon and the sun
Where real hearts beat
Animal instinct swirls with the grass blades
Hyena nuzzled at my feet
Polar bear yawning in sleep's defeat
Black stallion wandering aimlessly before taking a knee
Freedom underneath our toes
Gripping at the earth's heat
As we lie at the radius of where the sun and the moon meet

Twisted Parallel

Mental
Perplexed when it's so simple
Driving self insane
When sane makes you
Mental
Twisting your arm
How much can you take?
Twisted memories deep in your brain
Mental
Seeping poison through your veins
How much can you relapse
Losing your cognitive brain
Mental
Numeric letters on each side of your frame
Destroying your isosceles triangle
Parallel is each corner while shorting you to gain
Mental
Perplexed when it's so simple
Driving self insane
When sane makes you
Mental

Pandemonium

Chaos
Unraveling, ripping
Emotions gripping
Confusion, disorder
Breaking all borders
Shouting, screaming
Nonsense beaming
Gravity increasing yet erasing
Exciting . . . The chasing
Engraving chaotic storms
Feet stampeding
Normalcy creates
~ Pandemonium ~
Creates normalcy
Stampeding feet
Storms chaotic, engraving
Chasing the exciting
Erasing yet increasing gravity
Beaming nonsense
Screaming, shouting
Borders all breaking
Disorder, confusion
Gripping emotions
Ripping, unraveling
Chaos

The Man's Lyric

Bass draws the air thick
Two counts of eight
The treble goes up an octave
Setting the tone
For his rhythm to vibe with
Etching the stone
For his lyrics' hieroglyphs
Composed by a feeling
His voice placid
Purposeful words
The beat drops
His verse is toxic
Grab the ladies a fan
The rooms climatic
Stumbling on nothing
His flows problematic
Only pausing for the chorus to join in
Then the bass stops
He raps a capella
No acoustics
Gliding on the rhythm that he was born with
The treble ignites
BOOM!
The bass is caustic
There's sweat on his brow
But his tempo is so swift
It's crazy how these were just lines
On the width of the rubric
Now effortless gauge
On stage
Is the man's lyric

Through the Power Lines

Two best friends stare through the power lines
Gazing up at the sky
Watching each cloud pass by
Talking and giggling
About the who, where, and why
Time moving gradually
Mesmerizing . . . The blue of the sky
Capsizing . . . Reflecting the ocean's tide
Whether a midsummer's day
Or a midsummer's night
The time capsule flipped over
With a blink of their eyes
15 years later
50 states
1 on either side
Communication flatline
Not a beat
Not a pulse
Just memories and lost time
Now on opposite poles
Using opposite minds
Stringing together two different lives
Whether a midsummer's day
Or a midsummer's night
They both gaze at the sky
Two best friends stare through the power lines

To Sasha, If only I had a time machine to go back to then,
we would have never needed apologizes to mend
and we would remain unbroken, if only...

Angles

There you lay . . .
In your unconscious state
Devouring me completely
Though you're not awake
Wordless expression
Printed on your perfect face
Yet I lay six inches away
In awe of you and your warm embrace
Captivated by this angle
Sensual lengths
The width of your jaw highlighted by your facial hair
The indentation just above your lips
Perfect nose just under
Dark roast eyes
Pools of love from which I sip
I drink into you . . .
As you dip into me
Effortless body movements
Every limb dancing
Finding that perfect angle
As our bodies enlace
I'm absorbed into you
What a perfect angle to trace
Head tilted about 45 degrees
Due to the pillow
Chin held proud
Bare chest shown
A light bed of curls exposed
Where the blankets begin
One deep breath and you exhale again
Soft are the coils
As my fingers find their way to your hair
Silent love's whisper fills the air
You glow in the darkness

Your eyelids are closed
But I am well aware
Sleeping lighthearted
Though your desire pumps like a snare
Oh my, what an angle!
The slight separation from in between your plump lips
My breath becomes hasty
My hips begin to dip
Arching . . . their yearning
For your touch and more
The most forbidden fruit
And I'm Eve eating at your core
Do I wake you with sweet kisses?
Use my tongue to lick you into paralysis?
Leave you, my sleeping beauty
And transcribe each angle that leaves me in my wake . . .
Aching for your pleasure
Hypnotized by your embrace
Dwelling on this feeling
One must not hesitate
Grinning, a sly smile
From one ear to the other
I shall take you as my capture
I'll pillage
You'll plunder
Ravage with satisfaction
Undo to me
Undo to you
Undo to no other
The perfect angle from which,
We undoubtedly become one another . . .

Nightmare on Dream Street

(The Temptress Part 3)

Detective Anderson entered the medical examiner's office feeling a bit bewildered
"Lay it on me, Dr. Taylor. What can you tell me about our Jane Doe?"
"Caucasian, late twenties, about 160 lbs, brunette, blue eyes . . . cause of death is a bullet wound through her spine and exiting the sternum."
"Have we found an ID?," he muttered
"That we couldn't determine . . ."
"Her fingerprints were burnt off, I believe, from a very large match or a lighter. We took a mold of her teeth and sent them out. Results should be back soon.
Detective Anderson, her tongue was cut out!"
Detective Anderson scratched his head and let out a sigh . . .
"Was there anything under her fingernails, and what can you tell me about the knife wounds?"
"There were soil and skin cells under her nails. The skin cells matched the second victim, Gus O'Brennan."
"I'm not surprised to hear that. They did have a physical confrontation at The Tavern . . ."
"That's not all," Dr. Taylor continued.
"There are 12 knife wounds in total, all superficial, 3 above each breast and 3 on both of her inner thighs . . . We found spermicide along her vaginal walls. It's hard to say whether or not it was consensual or rape due to the condom, but there was no tearing, so sex did occur sometime before death . . . She was also 8 weeks pregnant!"
Dr. Taylor could see the dark intensity
That wavered over Anderson's face
Yet she could not know the intricacy
The unraveling pain
Deep under his surface
The jolting in his brain

Anderson cleared his throat before he spoke
"This murder was intimate . . . Perhaps by a lover . . ."
"Yet they left her in the street?" Taylor remarked
He replied, "So her body would be discovered!"
Dr. Taylor continued, "If they loved her so, why leave her naked . . .
Why not cover her?"
"Because," Anderson said dully,
"They want the naked truth to be uncovered!"
"Shall I tell you the details of Gus O'Brennan?" asked Dr. Taylor
"Yes, please do!" he regarded
Dr. Taylor pulled the sheet from the second victim
"Gus O'Brennan, Caucasian of Irish descent, 32 years old, about 200 lbs, redhead, green eyes . . . Cause of death is trauma to the head. It looks as though he took a very nasty fall!"
"And the burn marks?" asked Anderson
"There are 12 burn marks all together in formation of 3s, on his testicles, on his lower lip, on his chest, and on his hands . . . I believe they were made with the same object that burned Jane Doe's fingerprints."
Detective Anderson crossed his arms
And held his right hand to his mouth
Sliding his fingers against his lips
"It would seem as though he is no longer a suspect for our Jane Doe . . . Yet another intimate murder!" he remarked
"Yes, I would have to agree," Dr. Taylor continued
"We also found scratch marks on his back. These were given by Jane Doe . . . It would seem as though it was a sexual encounter, though he had no evidence of spermicide in the genital region, but I also found something quite peculiar . . ."
"Do tell, Dr. Taylor"
"His full frontal was saturated in bleach as if the killer was trying to erase or mask something!"
Detective Anderson's brows raised with piqued interest
"Very peculiar indeed . . . The killer left him hanging in the cellar by one foot. Just enough of him was visible to be found, but the rest of him lay hiding . . . Like a dirty secret, but then they cover him in bleach to wash something away . . . hmmm"

"Just one more thing, Detective. As you know, his ankle is fractured, the one that he was hung by. The opposite leg was twisted from the same fall that sealed his fate, but there was one more thing . . . His stomach contents revealed blue paint, ice rink blue Valspar paint to be exact! It would appear that both victims were tortured before being killed!"

Bells chimed from within Anderson's pocket

"Will you excuse me," he said

"Of course!" Dr. Taylor covered up Gus O'Brennan

"This is Anderson"

"Yes, Detective, another body has been found . . . You're gonna wanna see this!"

"Text me the address!"

"Yes, sir!"

Detective Anderson slammed his fist against the wall

"What is it!" said a fearful Dr. Taylor

"They have escalated . . . This case . . . This animal . . . has become a serial killer!"

Anderson mused through gritted teeth

Rage flourished on his face

He stormed out the examiner's office

Surely, this wasn't a coincidence

It wasn't a mistake . . .

Him getting this case

Baltimore

I don't know the Baltimore that you may know
Murderland
B-more
The bloods
The crips
The drug overflow
Never had yat gaw mein
Never heard of a chicken box while I was young
But now I know
I don't know the Baltimore that you may know
Never watched *The Wire* until about a year ago
Lived my whole life off of Reisterstown Road
I know about Maryland's beauty
The autumn, the snow
Chillin' at the snowball stand, the playground
These were the places to go
Playing in the creek
Cleaning up Mrs. Misterka's nature trail
Ask all OMES kids they still go
I don't know the Baltimore that you may know
The Chesapeake Bay used to sparkle
Now there's kind of a green glow
The county is turning into the city
More condos, less homes
Someone once told me they never had seen a raccoon
I laughed at the thought, if only they knew
I have more creatures in my backyard than you can assume
Raccoons, foxes, white-tailed deer, skunks, turtles, frogs, snakes,
field mice, squirrels, cardinals, blue jays, ravens, crows, rabbits,
chipmunks, groundhogs, praying mantis, crayfish . . .
So many that only God knows
If you change your 6-block radius
How many seeds could you sow?

Tearing down nature for buildings
Where do you think the creatures will go?
I can honestly say I don't know the Baltimore you may know . . .
Beautiful
Adventures
Life
Thrilling
Intelligence
Making
Overreaction
Reality for
Everyone
That is the Baltimore from which I have grown!

Fired

I woke up this morning
With an aching in my head
The meanest headache
Just throbbing in my head
I got up
Used the bathroom
Took Advil
And lay back in bed
And realized
The headache I was having
Came from the letter I was writing to you guys
In my sleep . . .
In my head . . .
I thought about my last words on the board
And wished I had gotten a chance to write this note instead:

"I took the job at TFM for the money. It was closer to home, and why would anyone who truly loved food *not* want to work in a bakery! I didn't come there for friends! But I can honestly say I found a friend in each one of you! That is what I didn't expect at the end . . ."

I don't want you to cry
I don't want you to be sad
A piece of my heart you have all taken
My time has expired, yes
But truthfully, it already was
I prolonged it to stay in your presence
I prolonged it cuz I wasn't ready to jump
They nudged me out the door
And I left just as I came in
Smiling and hopeful
But now I get to hold you all forever as my friends!

Detective Anderson

Like any good detective
In his past was a horrendous tale
There lay struggles and tragedies
His curse and his spell
And just like every other story
It began with love at first sight
Triggered by a loss
He was too weak to fight
He stumbled upon a case of
Blood and treachery
A case that wound him tight
Filled smoke in his lungs
Filled his cup with liquor most nights
Until the most beautiful women he had ever seen
Stepped into the precinct with tears of fright
Her twin sister had been killed, and she discovered her on-site
There she lay on the balcony
Naked, bound, and tied
Ligature marks on her neck
Though her neck was slit with a knife
No one should see a loved one like that!
Images of her sister's face haunted her at night
Detective Anderson helped her get through it
He was the protector by her side
Eventually one thing led to another
And they fell in love
If only he had said goodbye
Tragedy may not have taken her from his side
He came home drenched from a storm that blackened the sky
Two steps in the door and he knew something was awry
The balcony door was blown open
Off and on flickered the lights
Candles were lit in the kitchen
The pot roast in the oven was now dry

Flower petals mixed with bloody footprints
Led from the balcony to the bedroom door
He withdrew his weapon
Stepping lightly against the floor
He checked the balcony
The rain smeared the blood as it poured
He followed the footsteps that disappeared under the bedroom door
And when he turned the knob . . .
He saw the most heart-wrenching sight that ate at his core
There lay the love of his life
Her lingerie torn
Flower petals covering the cuts on her thighs
He ran to her, checking her pulse
Sobbing his love's name as he knelt by her side
He was too late . . .
She had already faded from this life!
There was a note . . .
Clutched in her hand, real tight
It read . . .
"This is only the beginning,
The end will come with your life . . .
Good night for now, Anderson
Too bad for your child and wife!"
It was signed with a bloody smiley face
Tears flooded Anderson's eyes
Little did he know
This was only the beginning . . .
Of nightmare's rise!

Moon Stars

"Give me the moon,
And I'll give you the stars . . ."
He whispered
As he stood on top of the mountain
Glowing against the night's sky
Overflowing with snow
Sparking like a fountain
Her last words repeated indefinitely
Echoing their love in his head
As if the words were pulled from her frozen lips
And echoed in the valley that lay ahead
He shielded his eyes
As the arctic wind laid blisters on his face
Providing hardly nothing except
Their memories first embrace
It was upon that same spot
Where he saw that twinkle in her eye
The first line of sight
She glimmered in the day
She sparkled in the night
On that day . . . ambrosia filled the air
Spring was in season
Flower petals lay in her hair
She swiveled and swayed
She twirled about
She had released the wild within
She had no cares
She had no doubts
He was perched upon a tree
Miles down from where he was perched now
He had been hunting for his supper
He was trapped in her presence
Until he saw a mountain lion on the prowl
The lion found her just as he had

Lying close to the ground
The lion was ready to pounce on his prey
When he shot an arrow right in front of its face
He pulled out a hollowed rhino horn
Making sounds to distract
Making his focus misplaced
He swung down on a vine
Grabbing ahold of her, sweeping her away
As everything glided past
They gazed in each other's eyes
He caught that sparkle that lay deep inside
He kept her balance
As they landed high above the branches
On top of a tree just below the other
The sun began to set
As they still gazed upon each other
The man forgot entirely about his super
"I am Astèri, and you are?"
A smile crept from the corners of her mouth
"A lovely name indeed . . . It fits you! I am Fengàri!"
"How so?" she remarked
"Does it not mean *star*? Though your beauty is far beyond that,
ma'am!" he muttered
"How sweet! No doubt you are the moon!" she flirted back
A secret passed from his eyes to hers
As if a myth had become real
Just as surreal as the knots and butterflies
They both began to feel
They absorbed the essence of each other
In that moment
In that space
In that time
Impeccable and mysterious
A new memory locked forever
In their minds
"If I give you the moon," she began
"I'll give you the stars," he finished
As love's destiny became clear

Raising his left hand
She proceeded with her right
Fingertips,
Palms,
Closed tight
He pulled her arm, wrapping it behind him
Without letting go
Reaching around her with his right
He placed his hand at the small of her back
Pulling her close
With her left hand, she grazed the scar on his chin
In awe of his afterglow
Retreating to grip the nape of his neck
Pulling his face to hers
Without hesitation
He kissed her swiftly
Pouring desire into her . . .
An echo of arctic wind swooshed through the valley that lay ahead
Fengàri shielded his eyes
Gripping the mountaintop
As the wind pressure hit him like a million snowflakes falling from the sky
He took one last glance at the stars
That blanketed the night
Knowing full well
There was only one star that ever caught his eye
"I'll find a way, Astèri . . . No matter how low, no matter how high!"
The avalanche split the mountain beneath him
And he tumbled right out of sight!

A Real Love Song

A true love song
Has piano keys
Playing out its symphony
A tempo that can tap into your heart
And sing out what you're thinking
What you're feeling
Rise above even Mariah Carey's highest note
And leave you reeling
Pull you from your world
And make you fall in love while kneeling
Make your heart race . . . No
Never stop stampeding
Make you stop trying to fit each piece of the puzzle
Because the puzzle now has no meaning
That real, that deep,
That burning, that amazing unconditional,
Inseparable love
Makes you hum each moment
Like there's no other emotion above
So true that you can't even believe what you're seeing
What you're tasting
A fool like no other
Because you can't even get enough
So rare that you can't even see it when it comes
A real love song spells out forever
Only echoing its vowels
Because there's no room for constants
Or that other stuff
In case the radio misleads you
This is what a real love song is made of

Nightmare on Dream Street

(The Temptress Part 4)

It was midafternoon when Detective Anderson took off toward
Ciliary Drive
His brow was perplexed
His brain going in overdrive
What would he find there?
What new crime scene would be engraved in his mind?
Locked away forever in the bank vault of his spine
As he sped around the corner, horror crept up his spine
The home was no stranger to him
A dinner party's memory saturated his mind
He parked on the curb and ran toward the entrance of the
cobblestone house
Praying to God, "Please don't let it be so!"
Almost knocking down a crystal vase by the doorway
An eruption of vomit started to peek in his stomach down below
He made his way to the kitchen
Where four officers stood stunned
As soon as his eyes lay on the body
A spiral of memories and tears began
Laughter, toasts, and singing all hit him at once
Echoes of a female's giggle
The female was once his first true love
Then a toast made by his lieutenant, his very best friend
Ending with a song of a sweet melody
Sang by his wife, Carmen
He silenced this haunting of happiness
As he gazed at his dear best friend
Lieutenant Micheal Clemin
Stretched out on the kitchen table naked . . .
Dr. Taylor entered the home, knocking into the vase just as Anderson
had
Startling the four officers, but Anderson was stuck in a trance

"May we have the room?" she mumbled
"Of course," one officer replied as they followed each other out one by one
The place was in disarray
Clearly, a brawl broke out in the kitchen
And ended there when the killer won
"Has anyone contacted Carmen?" Dr. Taylor whispered
Anderson let out a sigh and just shrugged
"I'll give you a moment before I get started and see if I can get in touch with her . . ."
And with that, Dr. Taylor left Lt. Clemins and Anderson alone
"Hey, guys!" Taylor yelled
"Check and see if the neighbors have seen anyone leave the home!"
Anderson surveyed Mike, realizing the horror he had been in
Vomit dripped from the lieutenant's mouth
His face was swollen
There was a foul odor in the air
His bowels had released
Diarrhea of despair
A drill sat a few inches from his head
12 holes were drilled into his body
From shoulders to knees
Each opening bled
Dr. Taylor dialed Carmen
She heard a hushed ring a few feet from the doorstep
Anderson turned away from Micheal
Looking around frantically, as if he misstep
He caught sight of a photograph
That was pinned to the refrigerator ahead
It was a picture of Carmen; her twin sister, Corrinn; and his true love, Kalenia
With a bloody smiley face drawn around her head
He flipped the picture over; there was a note that read:
"You failed the first time. I'm eager to see you fail over and over again!"
Dr. Taylor entered the house listening for the ring
Seeing the light reflect off of the crystal vase
There lay Carmen's phone, blood on its case

"Oh my god! Anderson!" she yelled
She leaped in the kitchen, watching him pace
"The killer's got Carmen!" she gasped
"He's got Corrinn too!" he mumbled
Rage perpetuated on his face
Dr. Taylor began to examine Lt. Clemin
As Anderson called Corrinn
"There's a blue tint to his skin, and he has hives! He could have been asphyxiated! Do you know if he's allergic to anything?" Taylor asked.
"Penicillin" remarked Anderson as he listened to the phone ring
Dr. Taylor located a needle that lay under the lieutenant's neck
"It seems as though the killer has done his research and is many steps ahead!" Replied Taylor as she held up the needle
The answer machine picked up Anderson's call
Though it wasn't Corrinn's voice, but the killer's instead . . .
"We meet again, Anderson . . . I've watched you suffer . . . I've watched you fight . . . But do you know any better? Now that it's time to save a life?"

Listen

I will listen before I speak
Open up my ears to hear
The sorrow through your gritted teeth
I'll be the envelop
As you write your letter with your tears
Catch them for you
Hold your hand as we walk through your fears
Pick you up before you reach the ground
Put the Love in Listen
When it cannot be found
Help you put down the knife
And show you the world that surrounds
I'll be the whisper when you can't take the roar
Show you the window
When they shut the door . . .

I will listen before I speak
I will not judge you
These words I keep
Put the Intellect in Listen
Show you the brain stem
Ignite your power
Make real out of make pretend
Open your eyes when you cannot see
Look for you when you cannot find the way
Be your Law & Order
Get you through the rape
Put the Strong in Listen
Show you how to fix it with more than glue or tape
Remove the bullet from you before you even wake . . .

I will listen before I speak
Show you the beauty you neglected underneath
Uncover the mystery of why

You are, who you are
Put the Tenacious in Listen
Help you travel far
Cut the cancer out of you and help you heal
Bring to you life's lessons
All answers revealed
Put out the fire before you burn out
Put the Energy in Listen
Wave away all doubt
Grab your hand before you can be taken
Lie awake with you
Hear your voice while you're thinking
Stop the car crash before you enter the road
Keep your soulmate's heart pumping
So you both grow old . . .

I will listen before I speak
Put the Need in Listen
This I will repeat
Release into me everything you feel
I will guard your letter
Permanent seal
Whispers to words
Words to roars
Roars to tears
Tears to fears
That's what my ears are for . . .

I will listen before I speak
You put the need in listen
You're strong, not weak
I have opened my ears
I will wipe the tears from your cheek
Keep hope alive in what you seek
I will listen while you speak . . .

Tormented

It's everywhere
You can't escape it
Reminders in front of your eyes
As well as in your dreams
Deep under the surface
You hide the pain in between the seams
Trying to move on swift
Affliction set aside
Then awakened by torment
Takes longer to forget
When the heart is famished
Trying to regroup
When the reminder is savage
Tearing you endlessly
While you glue every piece you can manage
You restrain the tears
But they have you at a disadvantage
Their weight is enormous
They mimic the ravage
Once you let go
You get sucked right in
Hurdled through the terrors
Reliving the torment from beginning to end
Time is the elusion
As the torment beckons
Dissecting your brain
Layers upon layers of hurt reflected
It's everywhere even inside
Labeled and inspected
You can't escape
From your head or your surroundings
Just hoping . . .
Wishing . . .
Praying . . .
For the torment to be vanquished . . .

POLICE LINE DO NOT CROSS

Breaking News

The city is on fire
15 buildings and 144 cars
Have all expired
Rioting and looting among our streets
Helicopters filming as our children throw concrete
Assaulting cameramen
Throwing rocks at the police
Who are these people?
Setting fire to our streets
Bloods
Crips
Black gorilla gang threatening police
While thousands of people march for peace
Social media shouting "Purge"
These adolescents swarming in fleets
Even adults are letting stupidity cloud
And create their own defeat
What is the message?
What is it that they hope to seek?
Freddie Gray
Michael Brown
Trayvon Martin
All black lives taken away
When will all see this is not why Martin Luther King Jr. paved the way
Yes, we need an increase in justice
But violence will only submit to decay
People grab brooms to sweep with strength
Trying to clean up the chaos of a Monday
Parents need to teach all children
To use their intellect to change the world of today

Dripping from the Canvas

Twirling the chiseled paint brush between her fingertips
She envisions the image she wishes to display on the canvas
Dipping the bristles gently on the palate
Absorbing each color full of metallics
Raising the brush, she begins with clean strokes onto the canvas
Manipulating the brush
Creating curves out of edges
Conveying a feeling with colored hieroglyphs
Transcribing emotion as the paint drips
Colors spill onto realities surface
Uncovering real beauty as the painting becomes elaborate
Suggesting a notion
Putting freedom on the tongue
While the eyes sip
Unlocking the immortality of the brain's passage
She signs her name with paint dripping from the canvas
Leaving her touch on the world
Wiping away the ridiculous
Opening the door for all artists
How a little paint can inspire courage!

My Verse

(RAP)

Although my voice is light
You can catch me sunbathing outta sight
Once the flow hits your tongue
I swear it's sunny delight
Skin the color of truffle butter
But the word skills are on tight
Twist the lid and take a sip
You'll forget what liquor tastes like
Beyonce will have you drinking
But I'll keep you sober for life
Aspirating its meaning
Forget the corrupt and misleading
That's how sex sells twice
I rather intoxicate your brain
While leaving on the light
Hit you with that old bay
You like that seasoned salt right?
Open the occipital
While you listen to that instrumental
Rehearsing like you wrote that song right?
I wanna see you scribble on that composition
Reflect on ideals instead of what's expensive
Put that Nike in your system
Just Do It!
Instead of partying all night!
Put down that reefer
Let the flow come out like ether
Let it reflect your frame
Go super sane!
Without pulling out a flame
Exciting the intellect
Grabbing respect

With the electrodes in your brain
She said, Naw not yet
but dude already came
That KABOOM became the thunder
And Durant ain't even in the game!
Connect the mind to the mouth
Then make it rain
That's how you start at the bottom
And become Li'l Wayne . . .

Nightmare on Dream Street

(The Temptress Part 5)

Detective Anderson sat hunched over at Dr. Taylor's desk
With his face buried in his hands
"The autopsy will take 2 to 4 hours, that's when we will know cause of death!" Dr. Taylor said
"Do you mind if I stay here? I need a quiet place to work this out in my head,"
Anderson mumbled
"Be my guest, there should be some food for thought in the fridge,"
Dr. Taylor answered with a shy smile
"I am deeply sorry for your loss, Joel!" She sighed.
"I am too, Holly. I am too," he replied.
Anderson ran his fingers through his thick black curly hair
Dr. Taylor's eyes swept over him once more before she closed the door behind her
"Why is this happening? Mike of all people didn't deserve this shit!
Now Carmen and Corrinn are missing? What is it that I'm missing?"
Anderson thought
He pulled himself to his feet and walked over to the fridge
"Food for thought huh!" He chuckled as he gazed in the mostly empty fridge
Nothing but 3 bottles of water, a half-gallon of orange juice, a pasta salad, a 6-pack plain yogurt, and a container of mixed fruits
He grabbed the container and returned to the desk
Leaning back in the chair he popped a blueberry into his mouth
He pulled out the victim's files and laid them out
What is the connection, he wondered
How will this all play out?
Static poured through the speaker on the desk beside him
"Anderson, can you come in here for a moment?" Dr. Taylor belted out
The chill of the morgue sent goosebumps up his arms
He stood stock still across the examination table

Trying not to give anything away, no doubt
"My assistant has informed me that our Jane Doe's dental impressions are back! Her name is Carolina Shall. She was charged with prostitution on the outskirts of the Optic Disk District. The paternity test results also came back. It turns out that Gus O'Brennan was the father after all!" Dr. Taylor remarked as she handed the file to Anderson
"Carolina," he whispered
"Tell me, Holly, have you noticed any similarities concerning the victims?" He questioned
"Each victim had 12 superficial torture wounds except the lieutenant. His wounds were caused by a 12V Black & Decker cordless hand drill with a half-inch HSS drill bit. All 12 wounds were through and through and occurred postmortem!" She swallowed.
"The killer must have been rushed . . . He didn't stage the scene like the others," Anderson said
"Also, the time of death for Carolina Shall and Gus O'Brennan is between 12:00 a.m. and 2:00 a.m. The lieutenant's estimated time of death is between 12:00 p.m. and 2:00 p.m.," Dr. Taylor declared
"Well, that isn't a coincidence. We need to figure out what 12 means! I'm gonna run to my desk. I'll be back . . . Let me know if you find anything else!" Anderson said with a weak smile
"Gotcha!" Dr. Taylor blurted out as Anderson was already halfway through the door
Not even 10 minutes later, Anderson was back in Dr. Taylor's office, slapping 2 more files on her desk
He engulfed a chunk of pineapple and opened the file on top
It read, "Karolina Deboise, 27 years old, 140 lbs, Caucasian, blonde, blue eyes, Cause of death is strangulation, time of death is between 12:00 a.m. and 2:00 a.m. Victim found on balcony with duct tape covering her mouth and bungee cords that tied her wrist and ankles behind her body. There are defensive wounds and signs of sexual intercourse before death. Parrying knife found in victim's kitchen sink caused lacerations on throat, above each breast, inner thighs, and buttock. 12 lacerations in total. Killer left no trace and is still at large."
Anderson quickly closed the file
Before his eyes lay on the pictures
Images of Karolina's death were already deep within him

Deeper than any suture
But the next file that lay before him
Was filled with even more torture
His heart stopped as he opened its contents
It read, "Kalenia Deboise-Anderson, 28 years old, 155 lbs, Caucasian, blonde, blue eyes, COD exsanguination, 12 lacerations in total, 6 on each femoral artery. Time of death is between 12:00 p.m. and 2:00 p.m. Victim found in bedroom with lingerie torn, no signs of sexual abuse, no signs of defensive wounds. Victim was 8 weeks pregnant. Victim held a note from killer in her hand, partial print found on jewelry box (item located on nightstand). No match found. Believed to be same killer as victim's late sister, Karolina Deboise. Parrying knife used for lacerations found in kitchen sink. Killer still at large."
Tears began to swell in Anderson's eyes
Now his best friend
Just about a year after his wife
Static poured through from the speaker next to him
"Anderson . . . I've found something!"
Dr. Taylor's voice trailed off
He wiped his eyes
Popping another blueberry in his mouth
Walked in to see Holly, saying, "What's all the fuss about?"
Dr. Taylor cleared her throat
"I found a note in Micheal's mouth! Here it is."
She passed him the evidence bag

With the blue letters peeping right through "First her sister,
then your wife, now your best friend, time is ticking
to save a life,
Who will it be Carmen or Corrinn? Either way, yours is sure to end!"
"He's after you, Joel!" Dr. Taylor gulped
"I know . . . Wait, this blue . . . I know what it represents!"
With note in hand, Anderson ran back to the desk
He opened each file that lay on the desk
He matched the note to the paint in Gus O'Brennan's tub
Ice rink blue Valspar paint, to be exact
Glancing from Carolina Shall, to Kalenia, to Karolina
It all fit like a glove
Those blue eyes he fell in love with
That sparkled even more than the sun
All 3 women had them
One connection resolved
Dr. Taylor burst through the door
"The blood results on Carmen's phone came back. It could be hers or
Corrinn's. It's difficult to tell since they're identical twins!"
"Okay, thank you, Holly . . . I gotta go!"
Anderson grabbed a bottle of water and grabbed his coat
"Where are you going?" Dr. Taylor stammered
"There's something about that note. That little old lady at The Tavern
knows something she hasn't told!"

Dip into Me

You dip into me
How a paintbrush dips into water
Saturating me with
Your bristles Your color

You dip into me
Like milk to an Oreo
Twisting each cookie
Licking the cream out the middle
Real slow

You dip into me
Like nachos to cheese
Swirling the chip effortlessly
Warming my body
Putting me at ease

You dip into me
Like toes to a pool
Spiraling me in your waves
Cool and refreshed
So in love like a fool

You dip into me
Like strawberries to chocolate
Coating me
Wrapping me gently
On the tongue erotic

Dip into me . . .

Home Run

We stepped to the plate
After stretching out our limbs
We were a bit nervous at first
As we dug our cleats in the dirt
Right under our shins
We raised our bat up high
Feeling our arms strengthen
Tightening our grasp of the bat
Feeling the wood become one with our skin
Staring through the pitcher
While making him think we're shakin'
Anticipating the curve
Estimating the speed
Unthreading the baseball
With the history were makin'
He winds it up
Releasing it with more power
Than Aroldis Chapman
Velocity clocking in more than 105.1mph
If we're not mistaken
The ball kisses the bat
As we swing with our all
The bat splits in pieces

The ball soars right through the air
As if answering a callin'
Right into the sun
Gliding right over the wall
We hit first base without fallin'
Dodged straight to second
Without stallin'
Ran swift to third
Rolling like Spalding
Sliding into home
Now that's ballin'
Leaving year 3 in the dust
Year 4, here we come
Now that's what we call
A home run win!

Nothingness

I lay here in the dark
Surrounded by memories and nothingness
Listening to my family breathe and snore
I lay here awake in their unconsciousness
Lost in the memories
Consumed by nothingness
Feeling the vibrations of the railroad
As the train goes by
Listening to the air conditioner sputter
As it bellows out cool air just below 75
Surrounded by memories and nothingness
Just as invisible as the air that floats by
I lay here in the dark
Hugging my blanket tight
Faint is the glow
Coming from the distant kitchen light
Enveloped in memories and nothingness
As my dreams hybrid pass the sky
Unhooking my brain
As the blood subsides
I lay here in the darkness
Surrounded by thought of memories
Drifting away
With the freedom of nothingness
I lay here in the darkness
Just me, myself, and I
As sleep invites me
One eyelid at a time
Nothingness

A Little More

Average love, you are not

Lighting the way, electric shock
Intense, satiable, irrefutable love
Tangible, fingertips of a whisper
Toxic, incurable even through gloves
Lullaby are your words to me
Every day expanding eternity

Mock me only in giggle's embrace
Obsessed with guilty pleasure's taste
Ravenous I am, though in love a little more
Even as I await each day's allure

Blind Ears, Deaf Mind

I remember her
That young girl
Just as naive as can be
I remember her features
As if she were in this mirror
Her eyes gazing
Straight through me
Wet blossomed cheeks
Where pain rained its dew
I see her just as clearly
As she should had seen you
But blind ears don't listen
And deaf minds don't think
Just the trembling in her hands
As the earth beneath her quakes
I remember her
That young girl
How the headaches wouldn't rest
A swift kick to the stomach
As her heart fell out her chest
I remember how she would panic
And would fall to the floor
Not being able to breathe
As she locked herself behind that door
Mascara stains and lipstick rings
Too many tissue rolls to count
But blind ears don't listen
And deaf minds don't think
Just the chill from the tiled floor
Hands gripping the bathroom sink
I remember her
That young girl
The screams that broke through her cries
The apologies that swarmed around her

As she was lost in an overcast shadow of lies
I remember how the questions
Were expressionless upon her face
As she gazed straight through me
I wished I could hold her, wipe away the tears' salty, bitter taste
But blind ears don't listen
And deaf minds don't think
Fist pounding on the door
As she barricades it with her frame
I remember her
That young girl
Just as pretty as could be
I remember her features
Before the loss became a part of her gaze
As she sat in her empty shell
Wreaking havoc on herself for days
She left physical for mental
Abuse comes in so many forms, so many shapes
But blind ears don't listen
And deaf minds don't think
Just the warmth of her diary
Where judgment has no face
I remember her
That young girl
Puzzled and confused
Not knowing what she did wrong
Little did she know
She was being used, manipulated, and torn apart
How devious and malicious people could be
This is not something that occurred to her
As she was trapped mentally
But blind ears don't listen
And deaf minds don't think
Boisterous are the hurtful words
As depression sits at the brink
I remember her
That young girl
As blood pumped rage through her soul

I gazed at her bruised body
The lifeless bulge of her eyes
Cuts in the worst places
Though superficial to her cries
I whisper to her that it will be okay
That it's only a matter of time
But blind ears don't listen
And deaf minds don't think
And the portal of this mirror
Doesn't go both ways
I want to raise my voice
And make this mirror shake
Distort her view
So she can see the beauty of this face
Show her the features that she's been gazing straight through
Show her that I see her
Just as clearly as I see you
But blind ears don't listen
And deaf minds don't think
Just the trembling in her hands
As the earth beneath her quakes!

Nightmare on Dream Street

(The Temptress Part 6)

Horrendous thoughts flooded Anderson's head
Nightmare's words echoed
Up Dream Street, he sped
"You failed the first time. I'm eager to see you fail over and over again!"
Was it too late?
Were Carmen and Corrinn already dead?
He came to an abrupt stop in front of The Tavern
The neon light flickered. It read, "Open"
He walked up the steps
The door was ajar
The Tavern was crowded
Only the little old lady behind the bar
"Hello, Mrs. Weston. Would you like some help?"
"Oh, hello, Detective, I wouldn't want to take advantage . . ."
"It would be my pleasure, Mrs. Weston!"
"Thank you, Detective. Please call me Glenda!"
Anderson slid off his jacket and went behind the bar
He washed his hands and turned into a barista star
He juggled shot glasses while filling beer mugs
He knew the difference in wines
Red, white, and blush
He kept customers laughing
Had women smiling like a schoolgirl crush
Forty minutes later ended the happy hour rush
"I'm so sorry, Momma. Traffic was backed up!"
"It's okay, sweetie. Detective Anderson was kind enough to help out. Detective, this is my granddaughter, April."
"Hello, April, nice to meet you!"
"You as well, Detective. I better get to work . . . Thank you for filling in for me!"
"No problem, ma'am"

April blushed as she squeezed by them to tend to the customers
Anderson cleared his throat
"Uh, Mrs. Weston, is there somewhere we could talk?"
"Just Glenda, dear. Let us have some iced tea in the kitchen."
"Thank you, ma'am"
"No, thank you. It's the least I can do for helping an old lady out!"
Anderson took a seat at the table as Glenda poured them both a glass and joined him
"Mrs. Weston . . . Uh, Glenda! I know you know more about what happened down the street than you let on. We were able to identify the body as Carolina Shall. Imagine my surprise when her last known address turned out to be yours . . . Here at The Tavern! Why did you lie to me, as well as withheld information from a police investigation?"
Glenda sighed and pushed out her chair
She walked over to her shelf of cookbooks
Selected one and handled it with care
She sat back down across him
And for a moment just stared
As if the space between them was infinite
Yet he was unaware
She pushed the book in front of him
Opening it at its folds
"I'm sorry, Detective, this is why I was scared! I found this left on Carolina's room door
The night she disappeared!"
There in the crease of the page was two ziplock bags
One held a parrying knife
The other a bloody smiley face drawn on either a handkerchief or a rag
"May I see her room?"
"Yes . . . Follow me!"
Glenda led Anderson down the steps into the basement
"Her bathroom is on the right, and her room is straight ahead.
Neither has been touched since she left"
Anderson entered the room, while Glenda stood at the doorway
"That message was hanging by the knife on the back of the door. I found it early the next morning when I was checking to see if she

came home. After I saw the police lights ricochet off the wall."
Glenda pointed out the knife markings.
Anderson took gloves from his pocket
Putting them on, he began to survey the room
"Glenda, can you tell me why Carolina and Gus were fighting that night?"
"I was awoken by a loud crash . . . It was coming from the bar. So I grabbed my husband's bat and headed down to see what was going on. I thought it might have been a robbery or something! I came downstairs into the kitchen and peaked around the corner. That's when I saw Gus and Carolina arguing and throwing glasses and chairs at each other! From what I could hear, Gus was furious about a man that she met with. He said he couldn't be with her if she continued to sell herself for money. He said he had big plans for them, and if she couldn't find a respectful job, he was done with her. Gus threw a balled-up paper at her and said, 'Or maybe you already have plans of your own!'
That's when he slammed the door and left. Carolina picked up the paper ball and stuffed it in her pocket. That's when she saw me and said she was sorry for the mess and she will clean it up. I walked over to her, took her in my arms, and told her not to worry about it. That I would clean up in the morning. We both stacked the chairs back on the tables, and she started to cry . . . She told me she didn't know what to do!"
"Do about what?" Anderson asked
"I don't know. She cried in my arms some more and said that it was a misunderstanding. I told her she needed to work this out with Gus! They were really perfect for each other despite both their tempers. She said I was right and went to her room. I went in the kitchen to get a broom and started to sweep. About five minutes later, she came running up the steps with tears streaming down her face. She looked as though she had seen a ghost. Before she could run out the door, I told her maybe she should give him some time to cool down and go to him tomorrow." She said, "Tomorrow will be too late!" That was the last time I saw her. If only I had stopped her, she might still be here . . . And Gus? Is it true? Was he found dead in his apartment?"
Glenda began to weep. "Yes, ma'am, I'm afraid so. We don't know all the details as of yet, but we won't stop looking until we find the truth, Glenda. I promise you." Anderson moved past her to grab her a tissue from the bathroom. As he pulled at the toilet paper roll,

something in the trash can caught his eye. All at once, a memory took hold of him. He was hypnotized . . . Officers swarmed the apartment. Flickering lights from the storm. Flickering lights from the camera. The click of the shutter lens. The slow drip of Kalena's blood hitting the floor. Anderson was so far gone. His ears heard nothing but the rain pouring. He watched as the ME looked over his love's body. How he wished she wasn't so exposed. There was a glimmer on the nightstand as the ME shined his flashlight. It was the latch of a jewelry box. Kay Jewelers, he supposed. He had never seen it before. He took a deep breath and arose. He reached the nightstand, looking at the jewelry box. It was the length of a bracelet, he supposed. He flipped the latch and opened it. A pregnancy test was enclosed. Now he understood the meaning of the killer's note . . .

"This is only the beginning,
The end will come with your life . . .
Good night for now, Anderson
Too bad for your child and wife!"

"Momma! Could you come up here? I really need your help!"
Anderson fell out of his daze
Nearly letting out a yelp
He gave the tissue to Glenda
As she began to excuse herself
"Thank you, dear. Take your time. Should you need anything, I'll be just upstairs!"
Glenda gave Anderson a reassuring smile
And headed up the stairs
He began to search her room
There had to be something in here that would take him straight to Nightmare
Who was the guy they argued about?
Why did she leave hastily up the stairs?
Why was tomorrow too late?
Where was the paper ball that caused all these tears?

The Hidden Jungle

Deep in the unruly wild apple vines
I found myself draped with beauty divine
Sun glistened through the treetops
Formations rooted along the forest floor
Walking along the deepest processes of his mind
Flowers in the shape of pineapples
Bursting with fragrant allure
Toucans flying high
Tree frogs in swarms
I close my eyes and listen
To the rush of freshwater
To the buzz of the insects
To the purr of the panther
Just a few branches ahead
And when I listen even closer
I can hear the whispers
Here where I stand
In the hidden jungle of his head
I can hear the stories echo
I can hear the hidden thoughts of his mind
Brains of beauty carved into the tree's bark
As I walk the canopy of his brain stem's heart
Understanding him fully
As I swing from the vines
Exploring each porous that is him
Eating the grapes of his wine
Swooning me with this rainforest melody
The pit of my stomach swelling me
Full of laughter
Setting me free of the shackles
Society gave me, lowering me
Deepening my fall into its abyss
He reached for my hand

But I grabbed at his lapels at the same time
Billowy are the winds
As I am now sushi to his seaweed
Wrapped in his earth
Tranquil in his leaves
Subduing me as we gaze in each other's eyes
In the middle of the rainforest
The deepest processes of his mind
Surrounded by the unruly wild apple vines
I found myself draped with beauty divine
Knowing there is no place above the treetops
In which beauty is carved into the bark quite like this
Understanding him fully
From innermost
To the outskirts
Fine, detailed edges
The jungle hidden in his mind

The Boulevard

Whether walking or standing on the boulevard
Time still passes by
Alone standing in the median
While the onlookers are in drive
Hypnotic are the vehicles
They are just colors
High beams of flashing lights
Unconscious to their surroundings
Unconscious to the pedestrian walking by
Footsteps leading
With syncopated tone
Where are they walking to?
Does anyone care?
Does anyone know?
Oblivious to their surroundings
While the person walking the boulevard
Is plugged into the unknown
Capable of reaching all destinations
Only after letting the steering wheel go
Attaching oneself
to the raw rumble of concrete
The steel in the boulevard's veins
As one lifts one's feet
Yet the boulevard is impervious to time
Whether one walks or stands still
The onlookers are stuck in drive

Detective Anderson

Part 2

A slew of murders brought chaos to the city
Victims from high society
To the scum of Dream Streets, gritty
Meticulous, how they were orchestrated
How random they would become
Nameless and faceless was the killer
Scene after scene of bloodbaths
Left the police department numb
Many officers denied the case
Passing it from desk to desk
Until it landed in between Anderson's thumbs
Night after night, he pored over the files
Searching each crime scene for any crumbs
He thought of the victims while he brushed his teeth
While he slept, he dreamed about what they had become
During the day he talked with their family members
But at night, he turned to a bottle of rum
Cigarettes overflowed his ashtray
Each one smoked down to the bud
The victims had not known each other
Let alone used the same body scrub
But there was one thing that connected them
And that is only the killer saw each one
Some of them were fighters
The rest were just completely undone
A mark was left in the middle of their foreheads
No one knew what it meant or what it was
Three dots that formed a triangle
Drawn with a permanent marker
Other than that, each time the killer wore gloves
"Yo, Anderson, you need some fresh air. Come with me to grab lunch!" yelled Lieutenant Clemins from inside his office
"All right, boss!" Anderson hollered back
Anderson put out his cigarette and closed his files

Grabbed his keys and met Clemins out front
"Where we going, Mike?" he said as he started the engine
"There's this new restaurant on the corner of Retina and Fovea. I wanna check it out before I take Carmen. I think I'm gonna do it there, bro!"
"Do what there?" Anderson replied
"I'm gonna ask her to marry me . . ." Mike lit a cigarette
"You're fuckin' with me, right?" Anderson chuckled
"Naw, bro, she's the one!"
"Yo, you've only known this chick 6 months. There's hella bitches out here. What makes her the one? You don't even believe in the one!" Anderson argued
"Look, man, this woman is the exception to the rule. I mean, I can't explain it. Everything about her lifts me to another place . . ."
"Mike, don't get mushy on me. Save it for her!" Anderson interrupted
Mike laughed. "My bad, bro. You'll understand one day!"
"Yo, I'm happy for you as long as you're happy. Real talk!"
"Thanks, Joel. You're the best man!"
"Thanks, Mike!"
"No, seriously!" Mike laughed
"You're gonna be my best man!"
Anderson busted out laughing. "I gotcha, bro, as always!"
They parked and walked in the restaurant
The place was called The Third Eye
It was one of those diners in the dark joints
They were greeted by two hostesses
"Hello, Detectives. Welcome to The Third Eye! I am Ally." The blonde spoke
"And I am Halley!" The brunette ushered
"May I take your jackets?"
"Sure!" Mike spoke up
Halley took their jackets and headed to the coatroom
Ally began, "This is our lunchtime menu. All you have to do is place your order with us, and we will escort you to your table, and your server will take over from there. At the end of your meal, you will be escorted back here to place your payment. Any questions?"
Anderson cleared his throat
"What's your favorite meal?"
Ally smiled brightly. "Honestly, I love the eggplant parmigiana."
"Okay, I'll take that!"

"And to drink?"
"Make that a beer for both of us. He needs one!" Anderson chuckled, patting Clemins on the back
"Very funny, Joel!" Mike said while gazing at the menu
"And for you, sir?" Ally asked
Joel whispered, "You can decide what chick to marry, but you're having a hard time picking a meal? Want me to call Carmen and ask her for you, bro?"
Mike busted out laughing. "You're full of shit . . . She decided for you! You know what, Ally, I'll take the same thing!"
Anderson laughed until something caught his eye
On the wall, at the top center of the menu, was the name of the restaurant, "The Third Eye"
The word eye was centered in between three dots forming a triangle
It nearly blew his mind
He walked over to Clemins who was busy ordering an appetizer
And whispered in his ear from behind
"I think we're going to get more than we bargained for with this meal. Up top, check your 9!"
Mike looked up over his shoulder and spotted the three-dot triangle, nodding his head at Joel
"Okay, all set now. We will guide you to your table. Your server will be Nigel!"
Halley spoke softly and grabbed Clemins' hand as Ally grabbed Anderson's
They led them into the dark, weaving left and right through tables
Seating them gently into their soft leather chairs
"Nigel will bring your beers momentarily"
Ally said, squeezing Anderson's hand
"Bro, how the hell you gonna propose to Carmen when she can't see you?" Anderson chuckled
"Don't doubt the skills, man. It's gonna be epic! Ain't this romantic?"
"Uh huh, sure, in a creepy kinda way!"
"Good evening, gentlemen. I am Nigel, your server. The best way to feel for your food is to keep your hands at the edge of the table so you can sense where I place everything. I'm putting your beers down now."
The glass bottles hit the clothed glass table at once with a slight ting
"I'll be right out with your appetizers," Nigel said
Anderson listened for his footsteps but heard nothing through the

shuffle of a group of women's heels behind him
"Mike," he whispered when he heard the women's chairs being pulled out
"I think this is the place!"
"I told you it was the place. Carmen's gonna love it!" Mike said aloud, gulping his beer
"No, you idiot, the place . . . The connection to it all!" Joel said as low as possible
"How long has this restaurant been open?"
"Here are your appetizers, Detectives. And to answer your question, this restaurant has been open for six months. Can I get you guys anything else?" Nigel asked
"No, thank you!" Clemins said
They listened for Nigel's footsteps as he walked away from the table
"Okay, Joel, I admit that was a little creepy!"
Mike chuckled
"Yo, it matches the timeline. I believe the Vics came here. That's gotta be how he picked them," Joel whispered
"All right, all right, let's see what we can find out. Now eat some of these nachos before I kill 'em!" Mike replied
Mike proceeded to unfold his plan of proposing to Carmen
As he and Joel waited for Nigel to bring their entrees
"Here are your entrees, Detectives, and I took the liberty of getting you both another beer. Now be careful, the plates are hot!"
"Thank you. Hey, Nigel, what does the triangle around the eye mean on the menu? We were just debating about it!" Anderson asked
"Well, as you know, The Third Eye is the name of the restaurant, and to some, it is believed that when one of your senses is blocked, it enlightens the rest of your senses. Being as though you are eating in the dark, you cannot see. Thus, it heightens your sense of taste, your touch, and your smell. Those are the three senses we focus on here, and there are three sides to a triangle. The Third Eye literally means enlightenment!"
Glasses shattered in the kitchen, followed by a woman's scream
"Enjoy your meal, Detectives. Cecilia must have dropped a hot plate again!" Nigel chuckled
"My gut tells me there's something up! I'll be right back!" Anderson said
He stood up, and it was like gravity hit him
He stumbled a little, feeling his way toward the direction of the

scream as best he could
Reaching the kitchen door, the light blinded him
He faintly saw a crowd of servers and cooks gathered by the pantry
He pushed through, stumbling his way between them
Hearing glass crackle under his feet
There, 2 feet in front of him, was a young black man with a slit throat bound by his feet
"The boy, what's his name?" Anderson asked
He was feeling a bit woozy
"It's . . . it's Nigel," said the young woman that screamed
"Fuck!" Anderson blurted out, trying to keep his balance
Clemins was still eating his eggplant when he felt a whisper against his right ear
"It looks as though your detective found me, Lieutenant. How fast can you move from your chair!"
Clemins scrambled to his feet, running straight into another table, flipping it on its side
"Anderson, out front now!" Clemins yelled
"Nigel, you can run, but you can't hide!"
"Mike . . . we've been drugged!" Anderson yelled
Trying desperately to steady his feet
Counting each step he had taken from his seat
Clemins smacked into a server while trying to find his way
Anderson fell over the table Clemins knocked into and felt a fork pinch his leg
Clemins made it to the lobby, his pace slowing as he stumbled to his knees
He faintly saw a server running into the street
He pulled his revolver out the holster and aimed for his leg
He got off one shot before falling to his face
Anderson came up behind him
Blinking rapidly, looking toward the street
He vaguely saw someone stumble to his feet
The fire hydrant was hit. There was water all over the place
He tried to focus, but he drifted into a haze
Everyone ran out the restaurant in a frantic craze
And that is how Nightmare was able *to trap* them in his maze

Entity

There is a force that is building with desire
Desire to transform words into something magical
Magically amazing and inspired
Inspire all people's ears to light up or even glow
Glow with enlightenment and enrichment
Enriching bounds of the unknown
Unknown electricity to ignite all brains
Brain stimulating imagery creating structures
Structures enticing all tastes, all flavors
Flavors unwritten to physically be felt
Felt by the tip of the reader's tongue
Tongues swollen from a force
Force that is building with desire
Desire for the written word to leap off of the paper
Paper to become an Entity

Moth to a Flame

Attractive and shiny
Too good to be true
Lights flickering at the end of the tunnel
While evil hides in the shadows
Waiting to take advantage of you
This American dream that they speak of
What can America bring to you?
So many cultures eager to place their feet in this melting pot
Eager to be free
Like me?
Like you?
Just wait until they find out
Just wait until they see
How America can rip your dreams from beneath you
Still a victim of society
If not professionally
If not financially
If not educationally
If not socially
Then *Law & Order SVU*
With so many treasures there comes misery
With so many scams there comes beauty
Even with explanations it's a mystery
Of why people do harm to each other
Whether purposely or conveniently
It neither bends nor breaks you
You are human
You have two hands, ten fingers to fix or change anything
Just like that moth going toward the flame
So hypnotized by its beauty
So corrupted by its game
You can still use the strength in your wings
To steer clear of the third degree
Conquering the flame with your reign
Then it will be you that's
Attractive and shiny

Nightmare on Dream Street

(The Temptress Part 7)

Anderson rummaged through Carolina's belongings
Anxious to find a clue
He bagged up the pregnancy test
And some Valspar paint swatches
Highlighted were baby blanket pink and ice rink blue
He sat down on the bed and looked around aimlessly
Until he noticed the vanity mirror was askew
He looked in the reflection at every angle
Trying desperately for another point of view
That's when he saw it
His curiosity grew
The corner of a book peaking from under the bed
He leaned down and reached until he could accrue
There in his hand was Carolina's diary
Aligned with rhinestones and pictures attached by glue
He flipped to the last page written
Inside there was a crumpled paper
Which Anderson withdrew
It read,

The Temptress

Come to me, my temptress
Shed your clothes for me
Tomorrow will be too late
If you wait, I'll take away your dreams

Come to me, my temptress
Reveal your filthy ways
Meet me in the street
Show your love you hide away

Come to me, my temptress
Even in death your blue eyes persuade
Tomorrow will be too late
Let us stop this silly charade . . .
Anderson stared at the poem
This was the crumpled paper that Gus threw
There were teardrops on the paper
They cascaded over the words
Creating an azul hue
Bells chimed within Anderson's pocket
"Anderson!"
"Hey, it's Holly. Is everything all right?"
"Uh, yeah. Dr. Taylor, I found a couple of clues. I'm about to head back to the precinct. Do you have any news?"
"I'm finished with the lieutenant's autopsy. Cause of death is anaphylactic shock due to penicillin."
"Okay, good work. Can you send a team to The Tavern on Dream Street. We need to check for fingerprints and to see if I missed anything else. Carolina Shall has a room in the basement here. I'm on my way!"
"Okay, I'll send them over now!"

Anderson entered Dr. Taylor's office
Handing her three evidence bags
But Carolina's diary he kept tight within his grasp
He laid the crumpled paper out on the desk
Opened the diary to the last written page
He began to read Carolina's last entry
While comparing it to her writing gauge . . .

Dear Diary,
Today has been such a mess. I vomited like a hundred times and felt a heaviness in my chest. Glenda caught me in the bathroom. Apparently, I worry her to death. I love Glenda though. I wish she was my mother (RIP Beth). So anyway, Glenda called April so she could fill in for me while I went to Save A Life. Gus has been really getting on my nerves about finding a good job. He thinks I'm still prostituting, but as a matter of fact, I'm not. All though today, I ran into an old client who would have given me a whole bunch of dough for some things that

Gus would never wanna know. I don't know what it is.
I love that big goof. He's the reason I stopped to tell the truth.
So I went to the community center where they sometimes have job fairs.
But right as I walked in, this stupid bitch spilled her coffee
all over my blouse. I was sooo fucking pissed,
but I threw up on her and my skirt before I could cuss her out.
So now I'm in my room about to shower and take a pregnancy test.
OH MY GOD!
WHAT IF I'M PREGNANT AND GUS DOESN'T BELIEVE ITS
HIS!!!!!!!!!!!! OH,
WHAT THE HELL AM I GOING TO DO??????
Wish me luck! Here goes nothing!!!

Carolina, The Momma!!! LOL

Anderson flipped through the pages
Looking for more clues
At the end of the book, there was a page that was missing
Actually quite a few
A jagged edge was left from them being ripped
He picked up the crumpled paper as if on cue
And wouldn't you know it, it fit perfectly
"Oh, Carolina what did you get yourself into!"
Anderson whispered as he closed her diary
His finger slightly stuck to a piece of glue
He decided to take the diary and crumpled paper to evidence
But took pictures so he could go over clues
On the desk lay several items
How eager he was to diffuse
He knew he had just a couple of hours
Until either Carmen or Corrinn were abused
He stared at the pictures of Micheal
The phone with either twin's blood
The picture left on the refrigerator
The message left by Nightmare himself . . .

"We meet again, Anderson . . . I've watched you suffer . . .
I've watched you fight . . . But do you know any better?
Now that it's time to save a life?"

"That's it, Save A Life," Anderson said aloud
He looked at the picture of the diary and read it out loud
"I went to save a life . . . finding a good job . . . So I went to the community center where they sometimes have job fairs . . ."
"Dr. Taylor, get in here!" Anderson screamed through the speaker
"What is it? What's wrong?" She burst through the door
Anderson looked at Micheal's picture
How the needle was placed under his head
Nightmare had a connection to everything
In all the items he left
He glanced at Corrinn's cellphone and the blood on the case
"Holly, there's a community center that you go to, to help Red Cross with their blood drive. What's it called?"
"It's called Save A Life. They're hosting another blood drive right now! Why what's wrong?"
Anderson reached for his walkie
"I need a surveillance team at Save A Life Community Center pronto. Nightmare will strike again according to our timeline. There is a blood drive under way, so take note of suspicious characters. We're looking for a male with deep British accent. I'll be in route!"
"Detective Anderson, this is Officer Smith. We already have officers on route. Our dispatcher just got a call from a security guard at the community center saying he found a trail of blood on the 12th floor. It was closed for renovations."
"Okay, have surveillance teams set a perimeter around the center. Hold everyone for questioning. Block off the 12th floor!"
Anderson and Dr. Taylor grabbed their jackets and ran out the door.
Anderson hit his siren and lights
As Dr. Taylor fumbled with her seatbelt
"Isn't it too early?" Taylor screamed over the siren
Somehow, Anderson thought it might be too late or so he felt
He wouldn't tell Holly that
He didn't want her to lose her nerve
Anderson swerved across the intersection
Sent wind blowing up a woman's skirt
Hit a right at the next light
Cut through construction

Dodging piles of dirt
Turned left during a red light
While Dr. Taylor's stomach swirled, she let out a burp
Two minutes later, there they were
Save A Life with the car parked on the curb
Five officers guided Dr. Taylor up the west staircase
As Anderson and five others took the east
Upon reaching the 12th floor
It was dark; electrical wires were showing through the ceiling
Blood splattered all over the floor
White paint on the walls were peeling
They followed the blood trail
As it left Dr. Taylor reeling
There was way too much blood for anyone to have survived
Where the trail ended, no eyes could pry
A pool of blood lay in front of the freight elevator
Only one knows what's inside
As blood dripped from a huge bloody smiley face on the door's
outside

To be continued . . .

In honor of Wes Craven
(August 2,1939–August 30,2015)

Tornado of Dreams

Image after image sweeps me up in its wind
Tossing me, spinning me
As the thoughts deepen
Violently, I tumble in the mind's whirlwind
Darkness surrounds
Nothing but 7 peepholes to peer in
I blow like a tumbleweed
Each hole I crash in
Helpless to the dream my mind suspends
Control is the illusion
Only conscious as the brain's puppet
The minute I take hold
I awake from the dream all of a sudden
So I shut my eyes
So I can travel back to the land with no doors
With only peepholes in the darkness
To which I am tousled
There are no bounds to the image on the movie reel's hieroglyphs
Sometimes no sounds, just me in the audience
Watching what I'm doing while questioning the choice of my subconscious
Other times the stereo blast, hitting every octave
In one night, details become so established
Emotions scale from simply happy to the tremors of terrified suspense
Pirouetting me into the reality of rapid eye movements
Lost in my own limbo
Created in my perception, my own abyss
Lying in my truth at my own expense
Arousal from temptation
The opposite of the life I live
Along with the demons of my own negligence
And when those appear, I awaken from the tornado I was in
Whiplash from the roller coaster of sin
So I turn over
Reeling myself back in
Finding another peephole of beauty that beckons
Derived from the architect's hands of my inception

The Soft Spot

There is a soft spot upon the lines I can't write
They turn into a squiggle
When I draw a dark, bold straight line
Even if I used a stencil
It would form a shape of its own
Filling in with ice cream
After I provide the cone
So subtle and invisible this soft spot would be
As it withers and wriggles from deep inside of me
Even if I used a ruler
It would fall at a slant
What is centimeters to inches upon my pencil's rant
No matter how sharp the lead
It would be swallowed from end to end
Defining and italicized
While changing the subject
Velvet and creamy
Chocolate drips from my chopsticks
No matter how it crumbles upon our lips
The soft spot is just glaze
That makes us stick

The Temptress

Come to me, my temptress
Shed your clothes for me
Tomorrow will be too late
If you wait, I'll take away your dreams

Come to me, my temptress
Reveal your filthy ways
Meet me in the street
Show your love you hide away

Come to me, my temptress
Even in death your blue eyes persuade
Tomorrow will be too late
Let us stop this silly charade . . .

White Butterflies

Once upon a time in the city of Rojo
There was a young prince
His name was Soho
He was rude, stubborn, and persistent
His eyes were black
But his skin was the color of cocoa
One day, the queen came to him
It was time for him to find a fair maiden
She would be hosting him a party along the bridges of Orinoco
He would only have until sundown of the full moon
Or he would lose his future throne to the prince of Poco
He searched far and wide
Upon every cliff and valley of Rojo
But he could not find one maiden that interested him
Nor were they if ever interested in him
Two days before the party
He visited his grandmother
She wasn't feeling too well
She was beyond bad weather
He spoke to her of his worries
Upon which she told him to visit the land of myrrhis
There was a princess to come of age
She knew nothing of his rotten ways
And if he was sweet, he could perhaps persuade
The princess to come to the bridges of Orinoco cascades
To watch the moon rise and the sun fade
Where she will be trapped forever
Even if true love evades
Soho left that night
Using the moon as a guiding light

Miles upon miles from the city of Rojo
Dancing under the moonlight was Princess Mariposa
She longed to leave myrrhis, but no, no
According to her father, it was forbidden
But she didn't think so
She had heard of the great legend of Princess Blanco
Who was just 13 when she left on a dream
To visit the bridges of Orinoco
It was there that this dream told her
She would have her first kiss
It would come from the heavens
And after she would lay an eternal bliss
Upon reaching Orinoco
The city lay hidden behind a great mist
Until a warrior approached her
His name was Con Negro
He told her we would help her reach the city
Actually he insist
He led the way of their journey
Upon each night together, they fell closer to one another
His aura became increasingly hard for Princess Blanco to resist
She told him beautiful tales of the land of myrrhis
He spoke of stories from Rojo
Filled with blood and clenched fist
They were yin and yang
Just as their names were opposite
Once they reached Orinoco and walked along its bridges
It was there that her dream came true
Just as the heavens opened, Con Negro placed the first kiss upon her lips
And after they lay forever an eternal bliss

Mariposa lay in the great field of myrrhis on the edge of the Great Lake
She heard a sudden sound of the water pushing and pulling at its weight
As she looked up, she saw a sight she couldn't believe
There was a prince paddling before her upon midnight's eve
A medallion of Rojo at the crest of his sleeve

It was the image she saw in her dream . . .
Upon midnight's eve, a prince would meet her at her special place
The badge of his city would shine upon lace
He would be sweet as a honeysuckle's taste
He would ask her to leave with him
To Orinoco, they would race
They would reach the city, and on the bridges she would gaze
All of a sudden all light would erase
Darkness would take hold of the entire place
Then from her dream she would awake
Even though the end was assured doom
She knew she was safe as long as she could see the moon
For there was a curse upon the princesses of myrrhis
If their gaze left the moon on the bridges
Evil would creep from behind the darkness, and for the rest of
eternity, there would never be bliss
Just as the dream foretold
Soho sweet-talked Mariposa to leave home
No luggage, no bags, just her white dress and hair comb
They sailed across the sparkling waters
Reaching the party at Orinoco's bridges
Just as the sun and moon began to switch places
The sun covered the moon; there was an eclipse
Once Mariposa lost sight of the moon, the world was covered in darkness
Evil crept from each corner of the skies, but
Mariposa wasn't worried she knew she had to make a sacrifice . . .

She kissed Soho swiftly on the lips
Then she dived off of the bridge
A few seconds later, thousands of bright lights took over the sky
Making the evil disappear, run away, and hide
The eclipse broke free
Everyone reveled at the moon's sight
Leaving Soho staring off of the bridge's side
The bright lights began to flutter; they came to life right before his eyes
That's how the world was gifted with white butterflies!

Blocked Out

Jettisoned like the wrapper ripped slowly from a candy bar
Peeling away the skin
As if being encumbered by tragedy wouldn't reach that far
Disposing of the scene's emotion
Blacked out as if given rohypnol
Subtle memory if any at all
Abandoning all recollection
Sealing damage behind a brick wall
Cementing the tears before they remember to fall
Until one day something scratches the surface of the unconscious
And fuzzy images appear like a dream
All the sudden you feel cautious
Did this really happen?
The absurd . . .
The monstrous . . .
The false stitching under the seams?
Or could it be anything but a silly ole dream
The puzzle doesn't fit when there are pieces missing!

The Twelves

At the twelfth hour
By the twelfth month
No blood had touched the blade
The thirst turned into hunger
A hunger no subsidence could aid
Strength turned into weakness
In weakness the mind concaved
Spiraling downward demons
Erupting with zodiac rage
Twelve dwarfs' worth of emotions
Twelve holidays engaged
Crippled by a flesh wound
Through and through
Swift as a turned page
As the fire hydrant exploded
I sought cover, giving me strength
To broaden my gauge
Twelve arises from twalif
"Two leftovers" so the Germans say
Yet this is literally only
After 10 is taken away
Just as twelve Olympians have risen
And Hercules enacted out twelve labors
Anderson is surely trapped in Nightmare's cage . . .

The Next Five poems
are from the year of
2007
That were found in a
lost notebook
That I felt should be shared
for learning,
smiling,
and laughing purposes!

Every Time I Ask

Why is it that every time I ask
You get an attitude
But when it's the other way around
I gotta reply
Because if I don't, suspicions arise
You would think a simple answer would suffice
But no, it's taken to . . .
A
Whole
'nother
Level
And if I ask myself why?
It could be the . . .
Past,
Present,
Or the fear of the future
Who knows only God!
Because every time I ask
You get an attitude
And every time I ask
All I hear is . . .
Exactly!

Once Were Together

Tell me . . .
Once were together
Will the compliments stop?
A year later . . .
Will you still claim I'm the best you've got?
Will I always look beautiful
Or will my smile make you frown?
Do I have to worry about
You chasing other girls around town?
Will you still adore me
When I lose my sight?
Running into everything,
Will you help guide my life?
When you say I love you
Will it always mean something?
Or will the meaning wither away
Like my makeup will do!
If my cooking gets bad
Will you still smile and say, "Tastes good"
Or will you tell me the truth
Like you know you should?
Tell me . . .
Once were together
Will things change?
Will you stick around
In our old age?
Tell me . . .
Once were together
Will you wish we weren't?
Will you tell me . . .
Even if it hurts?

Grandma's Love

How supportive is your family when there is a crisis
Or are they too worried about themselves
And not the patient's needs?
You would think that when something hits close to home
They would recognize the drama and hold their tongues
But with them, that is not true, indeed . . .
There's a grandmother in need of surgery
So 2 of her 3 daughters
Make the drive to see her the day before
With their 2 daughters and 1 son in tow
The third daughter lives at home
So she always has the info
They all deal with each other all night
Have a little fun and try not to fight
Until the morn at sun's early rise
They trample in the hospital room
With a little amount of time
To wish Grandma the best
With a kiss so blessed
Just in time before
The anesthesia puts her to rest
And she hasn't been in there long
So they wait . . .
A grandfather prays and reads his bible,
No less to give grandma strength and a surgery of success
While little boy small
The youngest of them all
Sits antsy, wondering why they're there so long
While Grandma's 3 girls are patient of all
The oldest sits and waits to be called
The middle one fiddles around on the laptop
And the youngest is being friendly and making small talk

While the only 2 granddaughters are all that is left
So they share a brunch at McDonald's
All time well spent
When Grandma's result is pure and successful
All can sleep tight
So in the morn, the granddaughters join forces
To make breakfast which ignites
Ignites the joy of a family
Of rebirth and laughter
So they take turns this time
And visit Grandma again
And this time, she has a joyous smile
And like always welcomes all in
When session is finished
They kiss her good night
For her bed supervisor will be there all night . . .

Any Other Nigga

Ladies!!!
Can you do me a favor?
Can you give me a **HELL YEA**H if your man has said
That he is not like any other nigga!
HELL YEAH!!!
AND PLEASE TELL ME WHY . . .
EVERY OTHER NIGGA BECOMES ANY OTHER NIGGA?
HELL YEAH!!!
See, ladies, we not new to the game, and we definitely know how to play it!
HELL YEAH!!!
So why is it that any other niggas don't find out that they were played?
HELL YEAH!!!
See, I knew an any other nigga once
Who thought he was that every other kind of rare nigga that us good women can barely find!
But let me tell you something, fellas
If you spend ya whole time tryin' not to be any other nigga
You just might be . . . any other nigga!
HELL YEAH!!!
See homeboy was on a good track
He was there for his woman emotionally
He provided for his woman mentally and physically
He even prayed for his woman spiritually
But one day . . .
The syndrome caught up with this rare kind of every other nigga!
And his sensuality for his woman was gone!
His timeless acts of generosity had disappeared for his woman . . .
And last, but not least
His intriguing aura was erased!
He was no longer a brotha, and you ask me why, ladies?
HELL YEAH!!!
He was down with another woman!
See, this once kindhearted nigga had now deceived his woman!

See, I don't know if you have heard, but our men establish us as 4
types of women, which are . . .
Wifey . . .
Boo . . .
Bitches . . .
And Hoes . . .
And I know you don't need me to explain, but guess what?
I know, you know there are 5 types of fellas, right?
HELL YEAH!!!
tHE mEN . . .
tHE bROTHAZ . . .
tHE nIGGAZ . . .
tHE bOYZ . . .
AND tHE SCUM . . .
HELL YEAH!!!
And homeboy just got moved to the last level
See, fellas once you deceive ya woman
You lose that mental,
That emotional,
That sensitive,
That spiritual,
That even physical bond with ya woman!
HELL YEAH!!!
Thus, this brotha played a game on himself called . . . karma!!!
HELL YEAH!!!
So this message is for all my men, my brothaz, my niggaz, my boys, and
even the scum.
Once you become that every other rare to find, where your woman's
heart, mind, and soul is always yours kind of nigga . . .
Don't become . . .
ANY OTHER NIGGA!!!

5 Types of Fellas

See, there are 5 types of fellas out there, ladies, and here they are . . .

The First: The Men

Now see, our men are the fellas we have been longing for our whole life. The kind of fella that understands and adores us by just looking in our eyes. The kind of fella that makes our hearts flutter, our spines tingle, and our cheeks turn rosy red with just one glance or mention of their name . . . that rare, hard-to-find fella!

The Second: The Brothaz

Now our brothaz could become our men quick! They are the type of fellas that our down for whateva when it comes to the girl. The ones that are there to help us feel better when some other fella has broken our hearts. The fella that will never leave our side no matter what! These are the ride-or-die fellas!

The Third: The Niggaz

See, this fella can cause us a lot of trouble . . . and will not give a flying fuck! These are the fellas that we tend to find a lot and will keep crossing our path until we decide to make them a brotha! These are the ones that won't leave us alone and will try at anything to get in our pants. Don't worry, a nigga is never hard to find . . . (P. S.) And they are always, always asking for money, a ride, or a booty call . . . Don't give in, girls. Stay strong!

The Fourth: The Boyz

Awww, boy, can't live with them and for damn sure can't get away from them! These are the type of fellas that feel like you **MUST** *take care of them. Believe me, you have seen them. The little boyz at the mall with their cheesy pickup lines. Like lost puppies looking for a new home. But don't worry, they will grow up and become ungrateful, ignorant-ass niggaz!*

The Fifth: The Scum

These have got to be the most annoying-ass fellas! They have no life and will probably only succeed at being our stalkers. These are the coldhearted fellas that will remember the moments you can't live down.
Yet you find yourself wondering if they are any good in bed?
(Don't worry, ladies, it's common. But they are still a waste of sperm!)
And remember if ya men, ya brothaz,
ya niggaz, or even ya boyz ever forget your number . . .
Don't worry, they can get it from the scum!
He's got it on speed dial. Believe me, it would be
#1 if it wasn't used for emergencies . . .
Right before Mom, Grandma, and niggaz!

"Upon finding this list of fellas, I realized I forgot one!"
The Sixth: The Experimental Nigga

See, ladies, this isn't 2007 anymore! There's a whole brand-new nigga out there! Just like there are many more names they call us!
Such as chicken head, thot, slut!
There are much, much more, but you would have to ask a nigga!
Right now, this is about the
experimental nigga!
This is the worse-upon-worse nigga out there! He's the nigga that moved up to be a brother, and somehow, he got your attention!
Now little ole you thinks you got something special . . .
Until you go to the doctors and find out
You got an STD from your experimental dog of a nigga!!!
And you ask me why, ladies?

HELL YEAH!!!

Cuz his ass was under the covers with another nigga!
And you wanna know why, ladies?

HELL YEAH!!!

Cuz this nigga don't know what he wants!
He has never known what he wanted and has never thought for himself!
And was told it was O-mother-fucking-K to make you the experiment!
It's not your fault honestly!
It happens!
Cuz this nigga will never be a man!
Unless he becomes a boyz man!

"Look out for the top 3, my ladies,
and stay away from the
bottom-feeders!!!"

Now Back to Our Regularly Scheduled Program . . .

Detective Anderson

Part 3

A couple of weeks had gone by, leaving Anderson nauseous
Confused on the timing
Replaying scenes in his mind
Of that day's events
Pissed that he was so close
Pissed that he lost him
Rohypnol on the rocks matched with a dark restaurant
Equals no image for a sketch artist
Fuzzy was his memory
As if still on toxins
Nothing but cigarette smoke passed through his lungs
Brandy flowed through his esophagus
Knowing that wouldn't help
But it did scratch the itch
As he rifled through crime scene photographs
Desperately trying to find a seam he didn't stitch
There were no eyewitnesses at the scene expect the two hostesses
They described a Caucasian male, average height and build, with short black hair Falling in the street
Before the fire hydrant turned explosive
Ballistics matched the bullet from the lieutenant's gun stuck in the fire hydrant
Upon which DNA was exhumed
Blood type B positive
Hospitals were put on alert for any gunshot victims
Five came in that week; none were a match, not even the description
Nor was there a match in the system
Anderson decided to call it a night
As he made his way out of the precinct
A beautiful woman pushed her way in with tears of fright
She looked frantic
Her behavior appeared erratic
She mumbled obscene phrases
Her blue eyes filled with panic

Anderson gently grabbed her shoulders
Stopping her in her tracks
"Ma'am, is everything okay?"
"She's gone! I can't believe she's gone! I just talked to her! Why is she gone!"
Tears poured out her eyes as she fell into Anderson's arms
"Ma'am, slow down and take a deep breathe . . . What's your name?"
"K-k-k-kalenia!" she managed between sobs
"That's a beautiful name. Kalenia, I'm Detective Anderson. Let's have a seat and you can tell me what's going on."
Anderson escorted her to his desk and pulled out a chair
Kalenia sat down burrowing her face in her hands and wept
"Kalenia, you're drenched. Let me get you something warm."
Anderson grabbed a blanket from the closet and went to Clemins's office
"Hey, Mike, come out here real quick!"
Clemins followed Anderson back to his desk
"Kalenia, may I take your jacket?"
She slowly shrugged it off, revealing blood on her sleeve
"Kalenia, there's blood on your jacket! Are you hurt? What happened?"
"I-I-I just got home. I was working late . . . I should had been there . . . The balcony door was blown open . . . I thought it was from the storm. I went to close it, and that's when I saw her . . ."
"Saw who?"

"My s-s-sister . . . She's dead!"
Kalenia broke out in tears as Anderson wrapped her in the blanket
Trying his best to console her
"Kalenia, what's your address?"
"20 Lens Apartment 3C . . . Why is this happening?" she whined through sobs
"We need a bus and CSU at 20 Lens Apartment 3C!" Clemins whispered in his walkie
"Kalenia, may I ask why you came here instead of calling 9-1-1?"
"I-I-I thought I heard something coming from the bedroom after I checked Karolina's pulse. I ran out and didn't turn back!"
"All units be advised suspect may be at crime scene or in the area. Canvas a 5-block perimeter!" Clemins whispered through his walkie
"Joel, finish taking her statement and meet me there!" Clemins said,

grabbing his coat before flying out the door
"Kalenia, I know this is difficult. I just need to ask you a few more questions. I'm also gonna have to take your jacket and shoes for evidence . . . Is that okay?"
"T-t-that's fine . . ."
"When was the last time you spoke to your sister?"
"Around 8:30 p.m. I called to let her know I wouldn't be home until about 4:00 a.m. I took another shift at the casino."
"Did she say anything out of the ordinary? Or was she concerned about anything?"
"No, she seemed normal (sniffles) . . . She was upset I wasn't coming home. She tried to get me to leave work (sniffles) . . . She said she ordered our favorite pizza and was gonna walk to the corner store to get some Smirnoff (sniffles) . . . I told her to leave me some. She rented one of our favorite movies, *Mars Attacks* . . . It's stupid, but we got a kick out of it, you know!"
"That movie is funny. I used to watch it all the time! Did you hear anything in the background?"
"Nope, she said she was home! She had the radio up real loud. She sounded like her usual happy self!"
"Can you think of anyone who would have wanted to hurt her? Or anyone she might have gotten into something with?"
"No . . . The only person she complained about lately was this customer at her job. She called her the Hat Bitch cuz she had a nasty attitude and always wore these big-ass church hats! That lady drove her crazy. She was there every Wednesday and Sunday! One time, the Hat Bitch went down the shampoo/conditioner aisle on one of those scooters and knocked everything off the shelves. It was a complete mess! I was in the store that day. I helped Karolina mop it up. We must have smelled like cherry blossoms for a week!" Kalenia chuckled
"I don't know what I'm gonna do without her!"
A teardrop rolled down her cheek
Anderson reached over and wiped it away
They stared at each other for just a moment
Anderson broke the silence, clearing his throat to speak
"What store did Karolina work at?"
"At World Gourmet on 7th and Fovea. She was a hairstylist at the organic hair bar in the center of the store (sniffles) . . . She was amazing!"
"One last question, did you notice anything strange when you walked into the apartment?"

"No . . . Well, the door was unlocked, but she often forgot to lock it especially if she was carrying groceries! I didn't really pay attention to much else until I saw the curtains to the balcony door blowing and . . . and . . . that's when I saw her . . . Naked, tied up . . . Duct tape was on her mouth . . . And there was so much b-b-blood!"
Kalenia buried her face in the blanket, trying to console herself
"That's all for now, Kalenia. If you could just write your name and number down for me, and I'll give you my card so if you think of anything or just need someone to talk to, I'm here for you. I'll do everything I can, Kalenia. I'm soo sorry for your lose!"
"Thank you, Detective," she whispered between sobs
"You can call me Joel, Joel Anderson. Do you have somewhere to stay for the night?"
"Uh . . . Yeah, I just gotta make a call!" She sniffled
"Okay, I'm gonna send CSU up to look at your jacket and shoes. I'll notify you when your home is released, and please don't hesitate to call if anything should come to mind!"
"Thank you, Joel!"
Anderson picked up the phone and dialed CSU
"Yes, it's Anderson. Send someone up to my desk to do a workup for Kalenia Deboise, thank you"
Anderson slid his jacket back on and pushed in his chair
"Someone will be up here in just a minute. I gotta meet up with my lieutenant! Are you okay if I go?"
"Yeah, go . . . My sister needs you now!"
Anderson squeezes Kalenia's shoulder gently
Until their eyes meet
"I'm so very sorry. I'll do everything I can!"
Kalenia nodded, and with that, Anderson walked away
He reached for his cigarettes in his pocket as he made his way to the door
He wished he could run back and hug Kalenia
Wrap her up in love's warmth
The same warmth that has left her core
He looked back until their eyes met
And then he walked out the door . . .

TO BE CONTINUED . . .

The Wine Glass

Life can fairly be compared to wine
Robust, sparkling, creamy, fine
Sinful droplets on the drinker's lips
Intoxicating as you sip
Empty promises lie within
Popping the cork, we all spill in
What we wouldn't give to have one glass
Slipping our fingers between its stem and bowl, simultaneously
Cupping its ass
So dirty! The grapes on the vine
A bitter taste yet sweet and sublime
Grabbing the bottle we swivel our hips
Tasting life at its fingertips
My, oh my, where have you been?
Saturating my tongue and skin
Shining brightly like that glimmer on the glass
Cascading from neck to shoulders to hips to ass
So dirty! The grapes on the vine
Life can fairly be compared to wine

The Whistle of Missiles

Here I sit alone
Draped in the darkness of the sky
Sitting in a lawn chair with a throw
As the whistle of missiles whirl by
An explosion of neon lights ricochet off the sky
Nothing but smoke
The aftermath that rolls by
Silence falls upon me
As if it never left
Lighting bugs caress the shadows
Accenting the forest cleft
The world whispers to me
As more colors invade the night sky
Sculpting its story
As a bat in the distance
Hangs on the figure 8 it glides
CRASH!
KABOOM!
Missiles dominate the sky
Vibrant hues violently disappear
Leaving me alone with my throw and my lawn chair
Draped in the darkness of the sky
Waiting . . .
Just waiting . . .
For the whistle of missiles to whirl by

This Damn Bird

One summer day, I sat outside to write some poetry
When all of a sudden, this bird started squawking
On the branch right above me
I really tried to ignore him
But he squawked insistently
My piece I couldn't write
Because no peace he was giving to me
I finished my poem in the house
So free from squawking I would be

The next day, I went back outside to sit under my favorite tree
There was no sound of him in sight
So I thought I would be free
Little did I know, a few minutes later
He would be squawking on the branch right above me
I asked him nicely to stop
And you know what he did?
He threw berries at me
And continued squawking!

About a week later, I set up my yoga mat
Back under that tree
I turned on my radio
Took off my shoes and started stretching
And just as the song changed
This damn bird started squawking
I paid him no mind, as the stereo was blasting
Just as I pulled one arm over my head
As I continued stretching
Something hit my arm and slid down to my hand
Something so disgusting!
I ran into the house screeching
"Mom is poop in my hair! Is poop in my hair!"
Thankfully, it wasn't
I would had took a slang shot to him
Knocking him straight out of the air

And right now, a few weeks have gone by
I sit under my tree
Staring through the leaves to the sky
I'm surrounded by nature and beauty
With my notebook and pen
Ready to write poetry
Thinking of subjects to dive in
But wouldn't you know it!
I can't seem to think of anything
No words, no phrases
Just this squawking rattling in my brain
Coming from THIS DAMN BIRD
On the branch right above me
"Why won't you leave me alone?"
"Why won't you let me be?"
THIS DAMN BIRD
So vigilant and determined
Insistent on annoying me!

There Is Blood on the Street

So many times have I felt life slip through my hands
Feel that last breathe on my skin
Watch as they fade into deaths quicksand
One second you're alive
The next your body tumbles freely
Ribs ricochet off tires
Blood splatter spills on to the street
This is more than climatic
This is more than sustained injury
It's death by his name
The name that he gets to keep
The driver never stops
Just as any coward flees
While you check the pulse
Feel the radiating warmth
From the loved one
From the dead one
That lies in the street
How quick they wash their hands of it?
It could never be that quick for me . . .
They just move on to the next STOP sign
While I watch the red bubbles slide down the pavement
Washing the remnants of their life off the street
A trash bag is a body bag
No comfort does it keep
One second we were smiling
The next . . .
There was blood on the street

To all 4 legged loved ones who never finished their walk in life . . .

Until Their Eyes Met

She leaned back into the darkness
As her hands gripped the chain-link fence
Rain flowed off the metal and dripped from her fingertips
His eyes are filled with wanting
As he closes the distance
Swift is his hand to her neck
His lips to her lips
Drenched into each other
Sweet cream of a Hershey Kiss
Rain became rapid, turning the surroundings into mist
Sliding off of each other, slipping hands to hips
Pinned is her back against the chain-link fence
Articles tear like coupons
Clothing too heavy for wet skin
Passion peaks from under her T-shirt
Soaked by the rain as his jeans she slides in
Now off onto cement
Closed off from nothing
Open to the earth right under heaven
Tennis court guarded though she's open
Nets begin to flap with the crack of lightening
Directional winds
Wetness explosion
She's climbing as he grips her wrist to the fence
Hoisting his anchor
His wooden plank she's walkin'
They are drowning at the ankles, knees, waist, eyelids
Wrapped into each other deeper
As rain bounces off the surface
Their moans harmonize with the stampede

of the clouds cumulonimbus
Swept away by moisturizer
Loves lustful abyss
Paddling to each shore
On higher tides even seen by Nova Scotians
Climatic is the weather
Physically intense
Until their eyes met
Through the smoke screen of rain turbulence
Neither her eyes nor his
Had seen love like this

Background Noise

Everything else is background noise
Compared to your concupiscent lyrics
One minute I'm sitting next to you on this earth
The next I'm dangling my feet off of a crater on this moon
Wild imagination though my heart is consumed
Lifted and shifted to the fourth degree of entirely loving you
No matter the fault in our stars
Flip through my pages and see how long it took me to find you
As if light refracted from my prism
On the other side of the rainbow there was you
Positioned at the right angle
As I slide off of indigo landing on a violet hue
Dreaming of the things that you say
Believing that they will come true
Watching the sky move in my kaleidoscope
Each and every pattern anew
As we lay above the clouds
Chasing the sun with the moon
Everything else is background noise
Unless the words come straight from you

Shinobi

She heard them whisper as she exited the room
Little did they know, they were right
Whether joking or they assume
Shinobi they called her
A ninja or covert agent of the moon
Powerful in body and spirit
But ninja qualities did include
Espionage, sabotage
Infiltration, assassination
Combat for all situations
As swift and stealth
As the change of her mood
A path marked by loneliness
Her body marked and tattooed
Even had an eye on her back
Before the needle pierced through
Always elegant and beautiful
As she picked through her men like finger food
Never sated each of them less of a challenge
Until her task would ensue
Finding her spirit beast
A phoenix
Rebirth through flames
That's how she sees it through
Though to them a concubine
Clothing more lavish than a prostitute
Though payment was mental
Broken hearts sealed by ratchet wounds
Cold to any lover
One after another
That's how she was looked through
Then she conquered nature's forces

Completing all tasks
Finally accepted true
Wind powered her wings
Fire from her beak
Left her victims subdued
The same victims that whispered her name
Yet her tears of healing raged
Sealed their open cuts like glue
Mocking the name
While living in emotions they couldn't elude
So caught up in her trance
Marked clueless to where her samurai sword would protrude
Bleeding, pumping heart clenched in her hand
Suggestive as she is lewd
Shinobi they called her
Shadow ninja of the moon
But wasn't it she that they pursued?
Hence how they amounted to nothing
But her finger food!

Angelou

Poet
Freedom writer
Soul definer
Singer
Rapper too
Like to say, "I am the next Maya Angelou!"
The statement however vague
Will never be true
If you are her . . . Then who will be you?
In her words . . .

"I don't ask anyone to win my freedom
Or to fight my battle better than I can.
Though there's one thing that I cry for
I believe enough to die for
That is every man's responsibility to man."

In my words . . .
She sang her truth
You and I weren't dealt the same hand!
Though I do wish I had met Maya face-to-face
But what is one surface?
To a grain of unshifted desert sand
Each word brings us deeper if not closer
Builds the ground on which we stand!
Her world plus . . . your world . . . plus my world
We expand
Creating an oasis
To give you a cool drink of water 'fore you die
Show you why the caged bird sings
And still I rise
No, I will never be Ms. Angelou
Yet my voice carries
Yet my voice sings

Yet my voice cries
Yet my voice is wise
I will illustrate a vision
Seen far and wide
Apologize for nothing written
Let my tears flow with pride
Leave my breast swollen
Phenomenal woman
Out and inside
I will not be hushed or pushed aside
The only movement is feeling
The only movement I can't hide
To Maya Angelou
Though you have returned to the earth
Still you rise
Whether by a voice on your words
The beat of a heart
Or the tear ducts that cry!

(Quote from *On Working White Liberals*
By Maya Angelou, 1928–2014)

Cotton Candy Clouds

My feelings are as soft as the clouds are see-through
Every emotion is painted on whether I hesitate or look at you
With your bullshit
Your ignorance
Your arrogance
Speechless of you
While my pink sweetness and blue calmness swirl in the clouds ahead of you
Then all of a sudden, idle threats and disrespect cling to my cotton candy
Sifting thickness into my clouds
And that sweet tooth creates a thunderstorm
Where the rain can't help but pour out
And if my tongue lash
Then that lightning strikes
I get cocky as I am proud
But that sweet tooth takes ahold of me
And the rain flows furiously without a doubt
I grow bigger
Become wider
Watch that F5 touch the ground
Destroying everything in my path
Do the math
Taking you and everyone else out
Until that sun shines
Creating a silver line
Wiping away all worry
Erasing all doubt
My feelings are soft as the clouds are see-through
Watch your bullshit
Your ignorance
Your arrogance
Stumble and fall straight through
Then those storm clouds go from gray
To swirling pink and blue
Never defeated but always sweetened
Dissolved I am of you

Graffiti

I will take this paint and spray its color on my canvas
Whether a building, wall, door, any asphalt tag less
Drip my color upon this black-and-white world
No need for outlines
Only abstract
No need for organization or furled
I will use this spray paint to highlight the world
There will be no gray areas
Just bold, bright, and swirled
Italicized
Overshadowed
Underlined
In the hands of all boys and girls
Put color to your words
Spread paint as far
As your toes and fingers reach
Ignite the match with nothing but speech
Break the black bars
Rip the white jackets

G ive
R eal
A rt
F reedom with
F reehand
I ndividuality
T alent and
I ntelligence

Take ahold of graffiti
And make it reality
Don't hold back on your canvas
Splatter it with actuality!

Police

That Black and White

All the features are black
But the chrome is white
Driving my Crown Vic like no policeman in sight
In fact, I've been saluted, even high fives
Saw a state trooper yesterday
He didn't bat an eye
As I sped down the highway
Doing 3 times 60
On I-95
You wouldn't believe what I have seen
The onlookers that pass by
Is she a cop?
I don't see any red and blue lights!
You make it so obvious
How suspect you look
The suspicion in your eyes
Makes me wanna write a ticket
Every damn time
Don't get me started on the handcuffs
That pleasurable pain
You know what I'm talking about
That Christian Grey
The sirens echo they lapse in time
Ricochet on everything
Make you halt in no time
This isn't Rihanna
That S&M
But if your baton's a li'l heavy
I can show you how to cut through wind
Report it and cuff 'em
That's how they break them in
To ready to say their right

Say they're wrong
They will hesitate . . .
Say that again!
So eager to find something
Slamming ashtrays on the ground
Searching your person
Yet no subsidence can be found
You serve the law
Yet draw judgment on each account
Now I'm not fooling you
I'm not fucking around
There are good cops that wear the badge
But where there is silence, there is sound
I see a taste of what they see
Driving my Crown Vic
Not dressed as a cop but dressed as me
I'm not a convict
Never committed a felony
Black and white isn't just seen on TV
I see a li'l of what they let go
Broken taillights
Weaving through lanes

Running red lights
Turnin' up bass
So you can't hear sirens ricochet
Speeding and passing with no signal
Think I'm making this up?
It's as real as it is illegal
There's black pavement
And white division lines
The median is what catches us
Taking or saving lives
No matter how you sketch it
White paper, black lines
There's a story to every case
Either you don't or you do time
Whether you're in the front
Or in the back
Or the on looker passing by
We tend to stop seeing color
And visualize in that
Black and white

Camera Lenz

Social media is on the rise
Their hands are hypnotized
With the steady click
Eyes locked, glued, memorized
Zoomed if not focused on social enterprise
Like they paid for it
When they pay for it
When the camera lenz is focused in between their eyes
They can tell you the whos
Whats, wheres, whens, and whys
Of everyone else forget yourself
It's the celebrities we immortalize
Like they're not human
Like the rest of you and I
E.T. Katy Perry
You wanna be a victim
Ready for abduction
They're the aliens
Their touch so foreign
It's supernatural yet extraterrestrial
Until tragedy hits the news
Yes, even LIVE
Let's go show the world
The worse of our human side
So they can claim its DNA
They don't understand you
Question?
Who was it really with the loaded gun cocked
Aimed to the side
Eyelids closed they can't see it
It did happen
Just a figment of our imagination
Realized and capsized
But when you gather the pixels

The image is exposed
All dark rooms are brought to light
How many times does Obama gotta say it
For your Oval Office to internalize
Our hearts go out the victims, and apologies
Are just sentences without the exclamation point brought to life
Yet the camera is still rolling
Picking up each echo of the soul that passes by
Social media is on the rise
All hands hypnotized
With the steady click, like, tweet, add, delete
We're only human
Just you and I

The Struggle

Sometimes you just wanna slip and fall in
That mountain you're climbing is getting heavy
That rock is slippery
You're stallin'
Reaching one arm after another
Pulling yourself upon a higher level
Jagged edges breaking through your epidermis
Bursting vessels under your skin
Blisters forming on your toes
Wishing you could dive off the deep end
But gravity is too heavy
Sweat from your fingers is drippin'
Conquering all hilltops
Just to be defeated by the mountain
Yet you push yourself to one ledge at a time
Heartbeat pulsating
Rhythmically you climb
Pebbles fumble from the soul of your cleats
The goal you are reaching still feels incomplete
Encouraging words stay on repeat
You're halfway there
The bungee cord snaps
Sweeping leverage out from under your feet
Frantically you tumble
Gravity increases the speed
Arms and legs flailing
Desperately grasping for something
Anything to keep distance from rock bottom
You smack hard into the side of the mountain
Your knees begin to bleed
You reach out
Stretching with the full length of your arms
Skinning your elbow
You find a grip to hang on

Your head is ringing from the prayers that leave your lips
Tightly you grasp the rock
A slight detour from your journey
The story won't end like this
Even more anxious as you stare at the top of the cliff
Dreaming of looking over the edge
Seeing the sun pirouette
Watching the sea wave its hips
Daydreaming of the dreams in your sleepless abyss
Steady you climb with more vigor than before
Not daring to look down
Unsafe with no bungee secured
Back at the halfway point you take a deep breath
Your fingers wither with each grip, each step
Mapping your offense
Too proud to misstep
Secure the footing on your right
While putting full weight on your left
Carefully choosing each rock
Before leaning on each ledge
BOOM!
Goes the lightning
The sky turns gray overhead
Shadowing your vision
Rain spills from the sky
Clouding your judgment
Slipping now that you're too high
But you proceed
You came too far to not try
Desperate to reach the top
Desperate to wave struggle goodbye
Finally you're face-to-face
One big leap to the cliff
Rain is even heavier
Limbs sore from the lift
You scan the area
Eardrums pounding with suspense

One wrong move and you could lose it
Hesitation ripples underneath your skin
It's now or never
The struggle only deepens
1 . . .2 . . .3 . . . Go!
No bungee, just you the rain and the wind
Damn, it's so slippery
But your hands snug on the tip
As you pull with all your might
Lifting yourself over the cliff
The clouds begin to part
The rain lightens
Sun rays trickle from the horizon
Now awakened
Daydreams turn into reality
From your sleepless abyss
Unfathomable scenes to be seen
The story ends like this . . .

Bow to Violin

I love the feeling
Your bow stroking the cords of my violin
Soaked up in your music
Lost in the kaleidoscope I'm peering in
Lost in the fluorescent dimensions you take me to
Star-crossed lovers
Bow to violin is me and you
Watch the ribbon glide on heartstrings
Emitting sounds slightly dark
Yet sweetly powerful
Punch drunk is the melody
Harmony whiskey sour

I love the feeling
My violin rubbed against your bow
Fingers slipped around the neck
Each cord plucked slow
Whispering soulful symphonies
Upon naked ears
Slip the world mickeys
And watch them all disappear
Toxins move swiftly
Complex muscles relax
Simmering with love
Each flavor extract

I love the feeling
Wooden frame against frame
Supporting the outer rim
While insides go insane
Accenting vowels
One language, one sheet
One stand, all bars
Hitting all notes
Stretching pass the world . . . far
Risen in all octaves
Deeper than baritone
I love the feeling

Violin to Bow

Slasher Movie

Tonight I'm gonna ruffle some feathers
Hand me a knife and watch me puncture the leather
People in my past still waiting for apology letters
But that's behind me now
I am who I am
Darling, trust I feel better
Excuse me, can you pass me a sweater?
Bitches got the cold stare
Call it hatin' on sunny weather
But I digress
Cuz my vocabulary is quite clever
They got the audacity to think I won't
But I will jump on nigga like Jack the Ripper
Strip ya and shred ya
Teach ya like master splinter
Butter my toast and spread ya
I can't believe it's not butter
I can't believe I even met ya
But God puts those in your path
To teach ya or provide the lesson
I'm not offended much
I got blessings on blessings
If Big Sean is deservin'
Then I must be respected
Resilient
Erratic
Spiritual
Protected
Ecstatic
Curvaceous
Talented
Educated
Dedicated

Much more to be expected
This isn't Marlon Wayans behind a Scream mask
I'm not gonna slash ya, gash ya, cut another hole in your ass
I'm a call up Micheal Myers as if it's Halloween
Hang out with Freddy and infiltrate your dreams
Matter of fact, I'm a take it to the extreme
Dig up, John Kramer; we call him Jigsaw on the blue screen
Or maybe give you a tour of crystal lake
Don't take off your clothes, here comes Jason!
One mask, no face
Are you corrupted by the angle?
Are you lost in between the lines?
Pick up the script and read it one more time
One minute your living
The next you're the walking dead
Bullet in the brain, no fame
While everyone else dies to be fed
Or maybe we should take it back
To Psycho, Jaws, even Lake Placid
Alfred Hitchcock's crows
Are you The Following?
I must admit . . . I was a big fan of Joe
Just look at how he interrupted
Edgar Allan Poe!
Don't forget Chucky
Dawn of the Dead
Edward Scissor Hands
The Headless Horseman?
Man! I could go on for days
I must admit those Killer Klowns did get stuck in my veins
Shout-out to Heath Ledger for his
"Why so serious?" face
I wish he could have continued
I wish he never left this place!
Why don't I wrap this up
So we can take you to your Final Destination
If you're worn from the feeling

Let me cut a hole and dig in
Nooo! I'm not a zombie
But I could devour your mind
Peel off your skin
Hand me that scalpel, please!
Yum, your blood is kinda tangy, yet sweet and quit fine . . .
Watch me suck on your bones
Gorge on the marrow while you weaken
Whoops! I snapped your neck!
I wasn't even finished . . .

The Masks We Wear

You ever watch a group of people
Lay their face in clay
Fire it in the oven
And decorate it an a misconstrued way
Painting it all pretty
Preppin' just to lie the night away
So all eyes stay on you
Fans flock to you
Watch them put stock in you
Just putting on a charade
While you sashay in your masquerade
Hiding your cunning eyes
Pickpocketing along the way
Absorbing every essence of value
Depleting value, watch your fans decay
Greed captured on the mask
That you wear so proudly on your face
Confidence building on the mask
Of your sadly weakened frame
Deceit is the truth
While your perception is a game
Latching onto every inch of beauty
While damning every sky gray
Try putting the mask down
And wear your face without the paint!

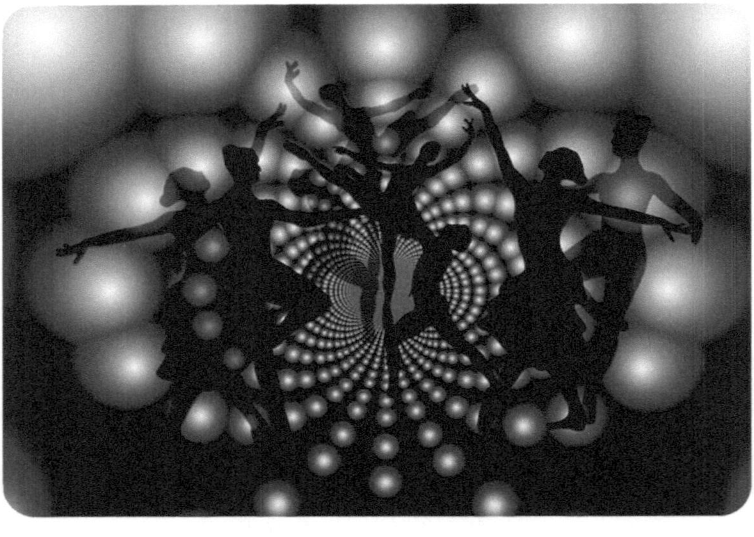

The Dancer Inside of Me

She's branching out to something spectacular
Using her body to highlight the vernacular
The rhythm is pulsating
Seeping into her foot's soul
Expanding through her veins
Watch her phalanges unroll
Each movement precise, as each action unfolds
Casting a mold as if the stories foretold
Quick on her toes
Each 8 count pours gold
Platinum is the star starring in this mirror so bold
Relevè
Pirouette
Arabesque
Rond de jambe
Piqué
Plié
Sur le cou-de-pied
Pas de bourrée suivi
Teaching French while on pointe, ballet
Tapping in your brain with step, ball change
Hop, shuffle, step, brush, step, ball change
Modern is the stance
The fetal is the base
Wiggle your finger while you move to the rhythm of swing
Jumping over your partner
Nearly knocking them offstage
Fan kick
Jazz walk
Pivot
Chassé

Whether stage left, stage right, up or down stage
The note is upbeat
Accent every feeling with rage
The tempo slows
To a ballroom waltz
At the height of flamenco
As sensual as tango
Whether line or single
She unravels her true self
Without one word spoken
The dancer is alive
Center Stage
Awoken

Float

I flow off the top
I flow off the feeling
Float like gravity
Straight thru the ceiling
You and I, four walls
No floor or ceiling
Can't spike the vibe
That sensual healing

Stuck on the words
Aren't they appealing
Open up your eyes while I leave your mind reeling
Keep track of mine
Echoes of me squealing
Watch me undress, see the weapon I'm concealing
Your flow is magical
Your thoughts, your revealing
Locked in my thighs
Every essence you are stealing
Wrapped in my spirit
This woman keeps you kneeling
Meet you down south
Up north you'll be wheeling
Hands on the game
What game are you dealing
Play the ace of spades
While my diamonds are beaming
Catch me on a satellite
Outer space dreaming
Stuck on your tongue
While your verbs are repeating

I flow off the top
I flow off the feeling
Float like gravity
Straight through the ceiling

You and I, four walls
No floor or ceiling
Can't spike the vibe
That sensual healing (2x)

I'm lying in your bed
While my mind you are feeding
Every orifice at the same time
Unpeeling
Dip goes my spine
Wanna tease me?
Get lost on the same vibe that I'm feeling
I'm thirsty for your love
I'm consumed by your lust
All in for you
No formalities, just us
You caught me by the hand
You caught me with your thrust
Power line drive, no hands that's a must
Intoxicated freely
Feeling on your frame
My brain you are kneading
Dough in your hands
Expanding each feeling
Pilot to my sane
I'll hold steady
Come and land this plane

I flow off the top
I flow off the feeling
Float like gravity
Straight through the ceiling
You and I, four walls
No floor or ceiling
Can't spike the vibe
That sensual healing (2x)

I'm floating in the stratosphere
Surrounded by debris
Debris of our love
Fingertips are melting
Four hands, two gloves
I'd ask you if you're ready
I'm never quick to judge
Hearts are inseparable
Upon beats tug
Real housewives of love
Surrounded by your essence
A true man's touch
Two lips you seal forever, no bluff
A real man sees a ring
No handcuffs
I flow off the top
I float of off your feeling
Once we lock lips
I'm the weapon you're concealing
You and I, four walls
No floor or ceiling
Can't spike the vibe
That sensual healing

I flow off the top
I flow off the feeling
Float like gravity
Straight through the ceiling
You and I, four walls
No floor or ceiling
Can't spike the vibe
That sensual healing (2x)

School's Out

What kinda world do we live in
Where blood-splattered condoms and needles
Can be found on our playgrounds
Bullies giving the bullied power
To raise a revolver without worry, without doubt
That's the world we live in
Gun license or not
Either aim for the head or aim for the heart
Letting pain and guilt rewrite history
Because you can't stand your own shadow
Taking it out on others
Because you think they might have a halo
School's out
No longer a safe haven
Students killed for stupidity
Students killed for anger
Student and killed shouldn't even be in the same damn sentence
Elementary terrorism
Young death
That's the life we live in
I can't tell you how to fix it
I don't know how it was broken
Generation after generation
Can't breathe the words spoken
Giving up as if life is the last token
Killing is a sin
A sin that needs to be broken
What kinda world did you grow up in?
What kinda world is it now?
Is it a world you can be proud of?
Is it a world full of raised doubt?
A world where we fight wars we don't understand?

A world where you're guilty even when proven innocent on the stand?
A world we want to raise kids in?
A world where we don't have to homeschool?
A world where we can go to the movies and
still be alive after 10 to play pool?
School's out
New games, new rules
The life we lived yesterday
Compared with the life we live today . . .
Just creates more fools!

Hourglass

Swirling through the sands of time
As each hour passes
The minutes drift by
Tick goes the tock
With these hands of mine
Gliding down the face
Of this watch of mine
You count down
While I'm counting up
Rounding off the top
Of what equals sum
Each grain slips through
After what is done
The rest is still swirling
Until their time comes
You can't stop the movement of infinity now
The minutes add up
As the seconds go down
Actions depict what the past repeats
Seeing the future start at your feet
The opening is small so it slows the pace
So you absorb with your tongue
Enjoy the taste
Opening your mind for the more profound
Looking at the sky while steady on the ground
The only difference between the hourglass and me
You can turn it over
Watch it sift the sand for eternity

Into the Propeller

Ripping off the Band-Aid just to put on another
Is like being a good person
While watching the bad suffer
It's like your heart is bleeding
For the love of another
Head warning of how sweetness can encumber
It's like walking head first into a propeller
The bad strike so swiftly
They leave your head spinning
It's like you're stuck without a paddle
While they're far out swimming
It's like using your heart
When your brain says, "Are you kidding?"
Giving the benefit of the doubt
When you doubt the benefit in the beginning
But the good don't think twice while their giving
Receiving isn't necessary as long as you have a smile worth grinning
Simple and effortless to giving anything for free
Treat others how you would want to be treated
And not how the past has treated thee
Encounter each person like their slate is wiped clean
But don't break your back just to give them your spline
Heed the warning of how sweetness can encumber
And try your best not to walk head first into a propeller

Remember Me

I want you to remember me
Remember me just as I am
Remember the sun in my smile
Remember the softness of my hand
Remember the love that pours out of my eyes
Remember my giggle
And not my cry!
Remember that I had something to say
Remember that I had a dream
And I own it!
Just a piece of me,
That gets to stay
Longer than this moment!
Remember me as you would,
Any sweet memory
Remember me
As if I spoke it . . .
I want YOU!
To remember me . . .
Remember me as a book left open!

www.ingramcontent.com/pod-product-compliance
Lightning Source LLC
LaVergne TN
LVHW041758060526
838201LV00046B/1043
9798886400137